"After taking an in-depth look into the life and times of the
WORKING WOMEN OF THE BIBLE, author Susan DiMickele beau-
tifully equips each of her readers with plenty of insight, perspective,
and too many "a-ha" moments to count—all while delivering a healthy
dose of humor as readers further identify with (and actually relate to)
their foremothers from so many moons ago. As history has proven,
and as this publication reiterates, God will continually call upon the
unqualified to lead, arming them for success in his name and for his
cause. 'Amen' for that . . . and 'Amen' for this book."

> —**Jenny Lee Sulpizio**, author of *Confessions of a Wonder Woman Wannabe*
>   (releasing 2013)

"*WORKING WOMEN OF THE BIBLE* is the most unique, refreshing,
and encouraging book about women and work that I have read in a
long time. Many believe in error that the Bible mandates all women
to work at home, barefoot and pregnant, with their only role being
to serve the men in their life. Susan DiMickele clearly illustrates that
God offers an incredible variety of work options for women of faith
. . . and he has provided women mentors from many different situa-
tions to guide us. Bible stories, personal experiences, and individual
reflection questions combine to create a motivating and challeng-
ing resource. The mentors you meet in this book will inspire and
empower you . . . and your work!"

> —**Terry Morgan**, Global Leadership Development—Campus Crusade for Christ

"Christian working women will be comforted by *WORKING
WOMEN OF THE BIBLE*. In tracing the stories of biblical working
women, Susan DiMickele reminds us that our struggles are not new.
We have all questioned the value, purpose, and direction of our work.
We have all performed tasks we deemed monotonous, while wondering why God has not yet provided us with obviously worthwhile
work. We have all struggled to glorify him in all sometimes
we are overwhelmed—someti   ourselves trying to maintain a   e
thousand-year-old stories of w
Eve helps steady our gait. With   n
continue our walk with God, kı   r
have been."

> —**Ashby Lawton Jones**, attorney and mother of two

"*WORKING WOMEN OF THE BIBLE* offers bold and inspiring encouragement to any woman in today's chaotic workplace. This talented author's insights into Scripture, woven with personal experience, offer hope and reassurance that women don't have to strive for perfection. DiMickele knows how tough it is being a woman in this male-dominated workforce. As a fellow working woman, I found this wisdom-packed book a refreshing must-read."

—**Donna Pyle**, founder of Artesian Ministries

"You were created to walk in love with Jesus, and designed to do good works, which God prepared for you to do.

WORKING WOMEN OF THE BIBLE will affirm your unique personhood, while lovingly challenge you to become the woman you were destined to be."

—**Harvey Hook**, Executive Director of The Gathering, Columbus; author of *The Power of an Ordinary Life*

"While the Evangelical book market has pretty much ignored the professional lives of working Christian women, Susan DiMickele steps in to fill the void with a solid resource, offering practical lessons drawn from the ladies who lace the pages of the Bible. DiMickele takes a different twist on some of those well-worn 'women of the bible' stories by uniquely approaching them from the perspective of a woman with a full-time job—one of influence and means—and garners fresh insights to share with fellow sisters who are sorely in need of inspiration and a strong spiritual pat on the back. This book is a delightful read: well-paced, insightful, encouraging, and based soundly in reality, rather than spinning soft Sunday School lessons. I can imagine the collective sigh of relief from working women everywhere as they grab a copy of the book and stuff it in their briefcases for a reassuring read on their morning commutes."

—**J. B. Wood**, author of *At Work as It Is in Heaven: 25 Ways to Re-imagine the Spiritual Purpose of Your Work* and *The Next Level: Essential Strategies for Breakthrough Growth*.

WORKING
WOMEN
of the Bible

WORKING WOMEN

of the Bible

TIMELESS MENTORS *for* MODERN WOMEN

SUSAN DIMICKELE

LEAFWOOD
PUBLISHERS

WORKING WOMEN OF THE BIBLE
Timeless Mentors for Modern Women

LEAFWOOD
PUBLISHERS

Copyright 2013 by Susan DiMickele

ISBN 978-0-89112-414-6

Printed in the United States of America

All scripture quotations, unless otherwise indicated, are taken from the Holy Bible, New International Version®, NIV®. Copyright ©1973, 1978, 1984, 2011 by Biblica, Inc.™ Used by permission of Zondervan. All rights reserved worldwide. www.zondervan.com The "NIV" and "New International Version" are trademarks registered in the United States Patent and Trademark Office by Biblica, Inc.™

Scripture quotations noted NLT are taken from the Holy Bible, New Living Translation, copyright 1996, 2004. Used by permission of Tyndale House Publishers, Inc., Wheaton, Illinois 60189. All rights reserved. Scripture quotations noted KJV are taken from the King James Version of the Bible. Scripture quotations noted NASB are taken from the New American Standard Bible®, Copyright © 1960, 1962, 1963, 1968, 1971, 1972, 1973, 1975, 1977, 1995 by The Lockman Foundation. Used by permission. Scripture quotations noted ESV are from The Holy Bible, English Standard Version® (ESV®), copyright © 2001 by Crossway, a publishing ministry of Good News Publishers. Used by permission. All rights reserved. Scripture quotations noted RSV are taken from the Revised Standard Version of the Bible, copyright 1952 [2nd edition, 1971] by the Division of Christian Education of the National Council of the Churches of Christ in the United States of America. Used by permission. All rights reserved.

Published in association with WordServe Literary Group, 10152 S. Knoll Circle, Highlands Ranch, CO 80130.

LIBRARY OF CONGRESS CATALOGING-IN-PUBLICATION DATA
DiMickele, Susan M.
  Working women of the Bible : timeless mentors for modern women / Susan DiMickele.
     pages cm
  ISBN 978-0-89112-414-6
  1. Women in the Bible. 2. Women--Employment. I. Title.
  BS575.D55 2013
  220.9'2082--dc23

                                                                                    2012045084

Cover design by Cover design by Thinkpen Design, LLC
Interior text design by Sandy Armstrong

Leafwood Publishers is an imprint of
Abilene Christian University Press
1626 Campus Court
Abilene, Texas 79601

1-877-816-4455
www.leafwoodpublishers.com

13 14 15 16 17 18 / 7 6 5 4 3 2 1

TABLE OF CONTENTS

For my parents

Cy and Stella Moore

ACKNOWLEDGMENTS

Writing a book during this busy season of life takes a village. Mine is especially large. I am blessed to have a supportive husband, three beautiful children, four older (and wiser) sisters, a remarkable agent, and a host of family and friends who have shared this journey. But there are two people to whom I owe my greatest honor: my parents. My mother and father are my strongest role models and dearest fans. They have always encouraged me to be the woman God created. Nothing more. Nothing less.

Thank you, Mom, for being the greatest woman of faith I know. And thank you, Dad, for showing me that the road to faith never ends. Your baptism at age eighty-two renewed my faith and gave me confidence that God is still in the business of redemption. My prayer is that we will never give up on God, because he never gives up on us.

INTRODUCTION

I f you're looking for a trendy Bible study for women, please move on. You will be sorely disappointed in this book. To start, I am not a theologian. I have no formal religious training, and I don't hold any positions of spiritual authority. So what business do I have writing a book about the working women of the Bible? It's a fair question that I will attempt to answer up front. But first, let me bring you up to speed on my journey.

To start, I am a woman. I am a follower of Christ, a wife, a mother, and a lawyer. I've also been working outside the home since my twelve-year-old son Nick was born, and I've lived the dilemma of the modern working woman. In fact, I even wrote a book about it called *Chasing Superwoman*. Yet, after I wrote my own story—the story of a too-busy mom, wife, and lawyer trying to do it all—I knew I wasn't finished.

There are more stories that need to be told.

Every woman has her own unique story. And the working women of the Bible tell some of the greatest stories I know. What kind of stories am I talking about? Stories of successes and failures. Stories of lessons learned and second chances. Stories of hard work and sacrifice. Stories of broken hearts and mended wounds.

Like many women today, the women of the Bible were trying to do it all: providing for their families, caring for the elderly, exercising spiritual leadership. Trying to be strong. Trying to figure out whether God can still use our work, despite our mistakes. Even trying to be Superwoman. It all sounds too familiar.

Those of us who have decided to stop chasing Superwoman—to let go of some unattainable standard of perfection—find that Superwoman is still chasing us. Superwoman is like a bad penny: she keeps showing up, like that permanent fixture in our rearview mirrors.

I think you know exactly what I'm talking about. Everywhere we look, our culture is offering quick fixes to our modern-day dilemmas.

Do you want to earn more money? Work harder and smarter.

Do you need to spend more time with your family? Work less and earn less.

Do you want to get skinny? Try a new diet and exercise plan.

Can't sleep? Take a pill.

Can't think? There's a pill for that too.

Overcommitted? Just say no.

Overstressed? Try yoga.

Undervalued? Try retail therapy.

We have a so-called solution for everything. And most of us are tired of these same old answers—answers we know don't work. The only problem? Once you decide to let go of the answers, it usually raises more questions. It's one thing to decide who you *don't* want to be when you grow up, but then you have to answer a more difficult question. Who am I really following?

As a follower of Christ, I do my best to follow Jesus. But let's face it—women need other women to help guide us on our journeys. As a lawyer, wife, and working mother of three young children, I still have to put one foot in front of the other and live out the daily grind. Sure, I know I am under God's complete and total grace, but sometimes I need some practical help. I need other women to look to—to pave the way on my journey. Working women need mentors, and I am no exception. As much as I try to juggle it all—home, work, marriage, kids—I often wish, "Could somebody just please show me how it's supposed to be done?"

I made the mistake of thinking my mentors had to live next door. That they had to live in my neighborhood, have my job, and have my educational and family background. It would also help if they knew what it was like to be married to my husband, raise my kids, and carry my load. Not to mention they should know what it's like to live in the twenty-first century. Could working women of the Bible—women who lived thousands of years ago—really offer workable solutions to my complex, modern world?

God has a way of providing answers where I least expect it. As I read about the women of the Bible, I realized the mentors I have longed for were right under my nose. Who needs Hollywood and Oprah when we have women like Eve, Huldah, and Lydia? Too often, we forget that the women of the Bible worked. And they worked hard. They made mistakes, and they didn't give in. In many ways, their stories are our stories.

So when Superwoman kept chasing me, I opened my Bible and started to read. I started with Eve—the first working woman of Scripture—and I kept reading about the other strong women in the chapters and books that follow. Many of these women are mothers. Some of them hold positions of power, own property, and flout cultural norms. None of them look like Superwoman. In fact, all of them seem to be different, and each seems to be used by God most when she embraces her own unique talents and destiny. Instead of fitting into a mold, each defies Superwoman with her own story.

After I read, I started to write. And *Working Women of the Bible* became my next journey. Thank you for sharing this journey with me. Of course, we can't study *all* the women of the Bible. Instead, we'll focus on the women who worked outside the home or held positions of spiritual or political influence. In addition to Eve, we'll study Rahab, Jezebel, the widow in debt, Huldah, Deborah, the Proverbs 31 woman, Ruth, Esther, Mary the mother of Jesus, Martha, Lydia, and Priscilla. All of these women—faults and all—give us insight and inspiration. All of these women speak to us as working women who live in two worlds: the spiritual world and the secular world.

I'm admittedly writing from a jaded, twenty-first-century lens. It's all I know. Please don't allow my words to speak for these women. Read their stories in the original text and test my ideas and interpretations. In some instances, I have attempted to fill the gaps where the Bible is silent without compromising the original text. In doing so, my words are incomplete and even presumptuous. Ask God to give you insight as you wrestle with your own conclusions.

If you're not sure whether you can relate to the women of the Bible, you're not alone. I wasn't sure either.

If you've stopped chasing Superwoman but don't know where to go next on your journey, please join me. We're about to meet some pretty amazing women.

CHAPTER ONE

EVE
The Trailblazer

Don't be too hard on Eve. After all, she has to go first.

Eve is the first woman to live with a man. Forget courting. The first arranged marriage is by necessity—Adam is the only game in town. Sure, it is probably pure bliss at first, even love at first sight. But after the fall, the honeymoon is over. I mean really over. Who knows if she is still in love with him? The habits she previously found endearing—like the way he talks in his sleep or cracks his knuckles—probably become nasty and annoying. Talk about being out of options. Like it or not, it is time for her and Adam to populate the earth. Together.

Eve is likewise the first woman to give birth. The first to experience the excruciating pains of childbirth. Without drugs. The first to nurse a baby. The first to hold twin boys in her arms. The first to beg God that they'd sleep through the night.

I've never nursed twins, but Shelly, my best friend from law school, tells me it's a full-time job. And Eve doesn't have a mother or grandmother to help. Adam is probably busy toiling the ground and hunting and gathering food. After all, Eve certainly doesn't have time to bring home the bacon and fry it up in a pan while single-handedly caring for twin boys. There are no day cares or nannies around, and I imagine that her first babysitter—other than Adam—is probably one of her young daughters, years later. Imagine never leaving your children with another adult. Ever.

Needless to say, Adam and Eve don't have many date nights out.

I don't know anything about going first. As the last of five daughters, I had little responsibility growing up. Someone always made my bed, served my food, and even cleaned my room. My sister Mona—like most firstborns—always claims she had it harder than the rest of us. Who could blame her?

Try being the oldest of five daughters with a strict, old-fashioned father. You're going to grow up fast. You're going to make waves. You're going to pave the way (and extend the curfew) for younger siblings who will thank you for years to come. And, like Eve, you're not going to get many date nights out—at least not without company.

Back in the early '70s, drive-in movies were quite the rage. Mona's suitors could only take her to the drive-in on one condition. She had to take *all four* of her younger sisters with her. Thanks to Mona, I went on more dates before age five than most girls will before they graduate from high school.

But even Mona would admit that Eve probably had it the hardest. Would any of us have done any better? Sure, she is the first woman to sin, but sometimes we forget about her other firsts.

Eve is the first wife, first mother, and first grandmother. But I'd like to focus on another first that is often overlooked. Eve is the first woman to work. And it was good.

PARTNER OR SERVANT?

God created Eve to work. In fact, God recognized that Adam's work alone is incomplete. Something is missing. *She* is missing.

> The LORD God said, "It is not good for the man to be alone. I will make a helper suitable for him."[1]

Is a helper a lapdog? Not exactly. The word "helper"—*Ezer* in the original Hebrew—means so much more than our modern English translation implies. *Ezer* is used throughout the Bible, most often to refer to *God* as Israel's helper in times of trouble.[2] Indeed, God is the only one—other than Eve—referred to as an *Ezer*. *Ezer* implies strength. *Ezer* implies leadership. *Ezer* implies action.

Simply put, *Ezer* implies work.

This doesn't mean Eve spent all her time washing dishes, doing laundry, or catering to Adam's every command. God doesn't create a servant, he creates an *Ezer*—a partner. Eve is expected to work. Besides, when you're naked most of the time, laundry doesn't pile in mounds and mounds like it does in my own fully clothed household of five where no one, except me, even attempts to conserve laundry. My husband, Doug, has a cleanliness fetish, so he showers and changes clothes about three times a day. The kids are no better. Between Nick's dirty clothes and stinky uniforms and Anna and Abby constantly changing fashion attire, laundry is the bane of my existence.

But not so for Eve. She has better things to do with her time. And if I read another book or hear another sermon on the spiritual value of laundry, I'm going to throw up. Laundry is a drag, no matter how you slice it. Eve doesn't have to do laundry, at least not in the days when work was good.

We'll never know the exact nature of Eve's original work. What does she spend her time doing, and what is the biggest part of her day? Do she and Adam divide and conquer the daily tasks—does he watch over the animals while she tends to the garden—or do they work in tandem, not needing to formally divide the workload?

We do know at least two things about Eve's work—it is *good*, and she is *equal* partners with Adam.

GOOD WORK

Most of us spend an inordinate about of time working. In fact, during our working years, nearly half of our waking hours are devoted to work. And we're working more than ever. In the last twenty years, working time has increased by 15 percent while leisure time has decreased by 33 percent.[3]

Yet few of us want to wake up and go to work on Monday morning. A staggering 97 percent of workers would quit their jobs tomorrow if they became financially independent.[4] Most of us don't *want* to work, we *have* to work.

And we're so busy with our daily routines that we forget to stop and ask, what is good about my work? What can I contribute that is of value to others, and what do I actually accomplish for a greater purpose?

I went to law school to pursue truth and justice. Sure, I don't always fulfill that mission in my daily grind, but most days I actually like being a lawyer. Even so, like the rest of the workforce, there are many days when I would rather be doing something else. In fact, when I start asking myself what is *good* about my work, it's easy to come up empty-handed.

Eve probably feels pretty empty-handed herself when she is kicked out of the garden of Eden. No more paradise. Work is going to be hard. She and Adam must toil for food and shelter. And she will carry the greater burden of the home—birthing and mentoring the children, being the first mother with no one to reassure her, "Don't worry, my kids did the same thing at that age," or "He'll outgrow that stage."

Even short of paradise, God still intends work to be good. Proverbs 14:23 tells us, "All hard work brings a profit." The Apostle Paul even says to "work willingly at whatever you do, as though you were working for the Lord rather than for people."[5] Yet if we're honest, most of us don't always feel like we're accomplishing the good work that God intended. Something has gone terribly wrong.

EQUAL WORK

God likewise intended that work be equal. God put Adam and Eve in the garden to "work it and take care of it."[6] Importantly, he doesn't give the charge to "fill the earth and subdue it" until Adam and Eve are standing side by side.[7] God clearly doesn't intend Adam to have superiority over Eve, but Christians are sometimes guilty of using the power disparity that emerges after the fall to drive a wedge between men and women, to justify the very inequities the church should be fighting against. And if we look all around us, things are far from equal.[8]

As a mother of young daughters, I hope and pray that they will have the same opportunities as their male counterparts. Yet my girls are privileged compared to the poorest, most desperate girls in this world. The global plight of women is heartbreaking—these statistics first penetrated my soul when I read *The Hole in Our Gospel*, by Richard Stearns. According to Stearns, women must first fight for survival and therefore have few options for meaningful (let alone prosperous) work:

> Girl babies are even killed in countries where males are considered more valuable. Those who survive are denied property rights and inheritance in many countries. In fact, women own less than 1 percent of the world's property. They also work two-thirds of all the world's labor hours, but earn just 10 percent of the world's wages.[9]

As a follower of Christ, a mother, and a professional woman, I wholeheartedly admit I'd rather not even hear these statistics. Sin has, again, thwarted the original intention of work, especially for women. Yet I am comforted by the fact that God intended something different—something more fulfilling (and equitable) for Adam *and* Eve.

WHEN THINGS GO WRONG

Things go terribly wrong for Eve. She screws up her work. She eats the forbidden apple in her own garden—the very garden she and Adam are in charge of tending—and the "good and equal" world she once knew disappears before her. Work becomes toxic. Work is forever poisoned. Work is anything but good.

To make matters worse, she screws up her home. Okay, maybe sin screws up her home, but every mother knows she probably blames herself when her oldest son Cain kills his brother Abel. Like most things in life, her personal tragedies are a combination of her own mistakes and circumstances outside of her control—like death, pain, and illness. But before we throw Eve under the bus—as some have done before—we need to appreciate and learn from her legacy.

Eve is the first woman to experience Murphy's Law. In fact, she invents Murphy's Law. *Anything that can go wrong will go wrong.*

So how does Eve respond? When she is the first to screw up, does she throw in the towel and give up? Does she crawl under a rock and refuse to come out? Does she quit working? Hardly.

She presses on through the pain and becomes the mother of all. Imagine how difficult it is to keep going first—always having to learn by trial and error and never having a mentor or peer to learn from. Yet Eve's fighting spirit makes her determined to continue the work God sets before her. It's not that she doesn't look back, doesn't have regrets, or doesn't question God's plan. Of course she does. But she keeps on going. She acts in faith, even though she will never see the fruit of her labor in her own lifetime.

The complete irony of the grace of God is this: God uses Eve's seed—Eve's perseverance despite her mistakes—to carry on a lineage that will one day redeem the world. In fact, he even plans it this way.

"And I will put enmity
    between you and the woman,
      and between your offspring and hers;
    he will crush your head,
      and you will strike his heel."[10]

God makes a promise to Eve. One day, her work will again be good. Through her offspring, God will bring his plan of good work to fruition. But Eve must wait—it will take generations to bring this plan to pass. Eve presses on to have many sons and daughters, including her son Seth. And the line of Seth makes its mark in history forever. Leaders such as Noah, King David, and Ruth are part of Eve's heritage. And, ultimately, Jesus of Nazareth is born to a virgin woman through Eve's seed. Who could imagine that Eve's royal debacle would result in such a blessing? Certainly not Eve.

LEARNING THE HARD WAY

Like Eve, we can expect things to go wrong—especially with our work. Workplace drama and disappointments come in all shapes and sizes. Workplace violence. Sexual harassment. Denial of promotions. Loss of job. Arbitrary decisions and discrimination. Downsizing. Backbiting. Office gossip. Office politics. Feeling underpaid and overworked. As a lawyer specializing in employment law, I feel like I've seen it all. Yet I'm always amazed at how work—work that was intended for good—can destroy some of the women around me.

When I recently met a friend I'll call Kate for lunch, I knew something was wrong. To start, she looked terrible. Like me, Kate's a working mom in her forties and we're both a little vain.

Kate wasn't wearing makeup and her hair was a mess. This was a clear sign that things must be *really* bad. Then she ordered a glass of wine at lunch.

It had been about eighteen months since I last saw Kate, and she had just landed her dream job. Kate had long been over-qualified and underpaid in her work, and a growing company recruited her to be second-in-command to the CEO. Kate was on her way to the top—in fact, she was second to the top—and her doting husband and two young daughters stood by and watched her climb the ladder. What could go wrong?

Enter Murphy's Law.

Kate's travel schedule became unbearable, and she barely saw her young daughters during the school week. Her husband moved out, and he started drinking again. He had just filed for divorce, and Kate was going to have an ugly custody fight on her hands. To whom would the court award custody? The absent mommy or the drunk daddy? Kate still loved her work and had decreased her travel, but she was working all day, every day. And the CEO she once respected was starting to take an unnatural interest in her personal life. He began monitoring her every move, even making sexual comments and repeatedly asking her to meet after work.

"Kate," I told her. "You're better than this. You have to get out. This job is destroying you. It's going to kill you."

Easy for me to say. With an unstable ex-husband and two daughters to support, Kate felt trapped. She needed her salary to survive. If she complained, she feared retaliation. If she quit, she feared she would be unable find a new job to replace her income. "What am I going to tell my next employer?" Kate lamented.

"That I was overworked and sexually harassed?" If Kate jumped ship too soon under questionable circumstances, she was unsure she could weather a black eye in the industry.

Like Eve, Kate's work was anything but good. Like Eve, Kate's plight was a combination of her own mistakes and circumstances outside of her control—a demanding career, a jealous husband who couldn't cope with her success, and a power-hungry boss who demeaned her as a woman. Like Eve, things hadn't turned out as planned.

Sometimes, work brings out the worst in us and everyone around us. At the end of our long days, busy schedules, and even broken dreams, it can seem unreachable to work "as though you were working for the Lord."

Like Eve, some of us need to learn lessons about work the hard way. But that doesn't mean we're going to give up on God. He didn't give up on Eve, and he's not going to give up on us. He certainly hasn't given up on Kate. And while I don't have easy answers for Kate, I can tell her with confidence that her present struggles are not what God intended.

He has a plan to redeem your work. And he wants to redeem you first.

Who knows? Maybe our present struggles and seeds of turmoil will bring about redemption in generations to come. Thanks to the many women of faith who have gone before us, we have a strong heritage. We have opportunities our mothers and grandmothers could only dream of.

But we don't always understand the journey. We often feel alone and, like Eve, we can't see the happy ending. And from our vantage point, we can't always see the plan.

I'm just glad I didn't have to go first. Like my oldest sister Mona, Eve gracefully paves the way for the rest of us. Thanks for going first, Eve. I wouldn't want to walk in your shoes, and I'm thankful you walked before me. We all benefit from trailblazers.

Discussion Questions for Chapter One

1. What is good about your daily work? Read Colossians 3:23. What would it look like if you approached your work as if you were working for the Lord?

2. Where has your work gone wrong? Have you ever found yourself in an unbearable job? If so, how did you respond, and what did you learn?

3. What advice would you give to Kate? Do you know someone who can identify with her plight? How can we avoid finding ourselves in her shoes?

4. How does Eve give us hope for the future? What if God took something you have blown at work—your mistakes and failures—and used it for a greater purpose and plan?

෨ *Select readings:* Genesis chapters 1 and 2

CHAPTER ONE NOTES

1. Genesis 2:18.

2. The word *Ezer* is used sixteen of twenty-one times to refer to God. The best explanation I have found of the word *Ezer* appears in Carolyn Custis James, *The Lost Women of the Bible* (Grand Rapids, MI: Zondervan, 2005). For example, on page 35, footnote 5, James provides a complete summary of these Scriptures.

3. Donald E. Wetmore, "Time Management Facts and Figures," The Productivity Institute, modified Tuesday, March 29, 2005, http://www.balancetime.com/articles/tm_facts_and_figures.htm.

4. Ibid.

5. Colossians 3:23 (NLT).

6. Genesis 2:15.

7. Genesis 1:28.

8. Even as a lawyer, a harsh reality of my profession is that women still lag behind men in pay, recognition, and opportunity. From 1994 to 2002, the percentage of female law school entrants increased from 45 to 50 percent—in other words, for the last twenty-five years, almost half of all law school entrants have been women. Yet, in major law firms, women make up only about 16 percent of the partnership ranks. Similarly, female lawyers are paid less across the board and hold fewer positions in the judiciary and in Fortune 500 companies.

9. Richard Stearns, *The Hole in Our Gospel* (Nashville, TN: Thomas Nelson, 2009), 156.

10. Genesis 3:15 (emphasis mine).

RAHAB

Second Chances

M ost of us take some pride in what we do for a living. When I first introduce myself as a lawyer, I sometimes get a negative reaction, a lawyer joke, or even a frown. But I can't imagine introducing myself as a prostitute. Can you?

It's a hard title to swallow.

Yet prostitution is one of the oldest professions known to women. And Rahab is probably the most famous prostitute in the Bible. On first blush, we pass over her story as entertaining but irrelevant. What can we possibly learn from an ancient prostitute?

Much more than we think.

To start, Rahab knows what it means to live in a secular culture. She knows what it's like to not be able to say no to your boss. And she knows what it's like to be stuck in a profession that doesn't value who she is. Talk about frustrating.

Rahab also knows what it's like to live life on the fringe. She certainly isn't welcomed among the high-society women in Jericho. She will never have a "normal" life. Nor will she have the simple pleasures most women long for—a husband, a family, a place to call home. She's the kind of woman who doesn't show up at church coffees and afternoon teas. Who would invite her? Besides, why would she want to put herself through all that shame? For Rahab—as for many women in the ancient world—prostitution is a way of life. What choice does she really have?

A Short Lesson in Ancient Prostitution

Before we get on our moral high horses and judge Rahab,[1] we need to remember that many people throughout the ancient Near East actually held prostitutes in high regard. Let's just say it wasn't a complete shame if your daughter ended up on her back for a living. I'll admit, I can't relate. Being a mother of young daughters, this mind-set completely freaks me out. I can't imagine a more degrading way for a woman to earn a living. But let's step out of modern Western culture for a moment and look at the world through Rahab's eyes.

In Rahab's world, not all prostitutes are created equal. At least two types of prostitution are mentioned in the Bible: (1) ritual prostitutes and (2) commercial prostitutes. Ritual prostitutes (also called temple prostitutes) are held in higher regard than their commercial counterparts. Men frequent the pagan temples and offer "donations" in exchange for sex with ritual prostitutes, in honor of fertility gods. Talk about a religious scam—casual sex in the name of worship! Ritual prostitution makes some of our modern-day televangelist schemes look like child's play.

Commercial prostitution, however, is much less glamorous. There are no religious overtones or sugarcoating of intentions. It's simply sex for money. Period. Not surprising, archaeological studies show commercial prostitution common in drinking establishments and inns. Because Rahab is also an innkeeper, this leads me to believe she is likely a commercial prostitute (or a combination of the two). But we'll never know for sure.

What we do know is that Rahab is probably a respectable businesswoman. While some scholars claim she was just an "innkeeper" I tend to take her story at face value. Like many women before her and after her, Rahab uses her sexuality to gain an advantage in the business world. Sound familiar?

Before we move on, please don't misunderstand me. I'm not saying that prostitution is acceptable in Rahab's circumstances. While prostitution many have been normal in her ancient culture, it was certainly forbidden by the Jews. And I personally believe it was despicable to Rahab. Like most women stuck in this cycle, she is likely looking (and praying) for a way out.

So Much More Than a Prostitute

If we think Rahab is just a prostitute, we miss everything. Rahab is undoubtedly a woman with talents and dreams. And, like many of us, she carries the weight of the world on her shoulders. This includes wearing multiple hats of caregiver, homemaker, property owner, business owner, and political insider. Even before Rahab is rescued from Jericho, she is so much more than a prostitute.

First and foremost, Rahab is a caregiver. She supports not only her aging parents but her extended family and siblings. There is no mention of a husband or children—not surprising given her lifestyle. This means she has all of the burdens of a family without the benefits. After a hard day's work, she doesn't get to hold her children or recline with her husband for the evening. Instead, she shares a bed with a stranger and wakes up alone.

As the family provider, it's not like Rahab can say, *Hey, I'm going back to school* or *I'm going to head out west and look for new work.* She likely feels stuck—that there is no way out. After all, who else will care for her family? Someone has to do it.

A homeowner (and property owner), Rahab is responsible not only for food and shelter but also for the upkeep and maintenance of her inn. She probably has to fix her own faucet and hang her own wallpaper. She takes out her own trash and has her own tool belt. And Rahab appears to be the leader of her family. When she learns of the imminent fall of Jericho, she takes charge as the family protector. Rahab's role of provider and protector makes her close to the heart of a growing population of single women who are the head of household, often caring for extended family and aging parents.

CAN SHE WORK ANY HARDER?

It sounds like too much for one woman to handle. But we're still not done. Rahab is also a political woman. This may stem from the fact that her house is in a well-protected strategic location—likely situated in a fifteen-foot gap between the double walls of ancient Jericho. She serves as a "protector" of the city and advisor to the king. Clearly, she is in the king's trusted circle and under his microscope. It's not like she shouts to the king, *I have some Israelite spies hanging out in the inn.* No, the king already knows about her unexpected visitors. He is watching her every move, and she can't get away with anything. Talk about pressure to perform.

Rahab also runs *multiple* businesses. In addition to being a prostitute, an innkeeper, and an advisor to the king, she has yet another side business in fine linens. Rahab stores and dries flax on her flat roof. This shows us she is industrious and even entrepreneurial. Perhaps she also weaves linen from the flax and sells it in the marketplace. No doubt, Rahab has the raw materials for a modern leader in business. She is no stranger to the 24/7 work ethic. I get exhausted just watching her. She obviously doesn't sleep.

Like any lousy job, Rahab's work has its benefits. First and foremost, she is turning a healthy profit. She has multiple sources of income. She is in charge. She has resources. Maybe she even has respect. And she is connected at the highest levels of her community.

But prostitution degrades the very core of Rahab's being. And while most work has its benefits, I believe that Rahab is utterly and completely miserable. That she begged God every night for a way out. For a new life. That one day she would wake up from the nightmare.

ONCE A PROSTITUTE, ALWAYS A PROSTITUTE?

Rahab must have heard these words over and over again in her mind: *Rahab, you are a prostitute. You will never be anything more. You are Rahab the Prostitute—with a capital P!*

Can you imagine the pain or emotional torture? I can't. I don't even know any prostitutes. While I've supported organizations that fight human trafficking, I am completely and totally unqualified to discuss the psychological, physical, and spiritual implications of prostitution on women.

So I won't even try. Instead, I'd like to look at Rahab in a different light. I don't mean to overlook or minimize her lifestyle, but I see Rahab as a sinner. Pure and simple. Just like you and me. Yeah, she's stuck in a really *nasty* cycle of sin. But is there any other kind? Some of it is probably her fault. Some of it isn't. But I'm not going to worry about how she got there. Instead, I'd like to focus on her remarkable journey of getting out!

Deep down, Rahab knows she is more than a prostitute. So she doesn't allow prostitution to define who she is. While it may have defined her past, it doesn't define her future. Instead of listening to the voices that say *you are Rahab the Prostitute*, she moves beyond the here and now. She reaches for a better life. She's not afraid to hope.

Rahab's story of deliverance is relevant to any woman who *needs* to make a change, yet doesn't know where to start. She teaches us a modern-day course in change management. What's her secret? She has mastered the three Rs—readiness, risk, and regret. She is ready, she risks everything, and she doesn't regret. I love her simple yet profound formula.

THE POWER OF READINESS

Most of us completely underestimate the power of readiness. We're so busy thinking about how badly we *want* a change that we forget to be *ready* for change. Wanting gets us nowhere. Wanting is about being passive and blaming others for our circumstances. Readiness is just the opposite. It's about moving beyond our circumstances and engaging in action. It involves anticipation and preparation.

Rahab demonstrates this type of readiness. When the Israelite spies descend upon her home, she acts quickly and decisively to prevent their capture. She doesn't mess around with indecision. She doesn't lack resources. Instead, she acts swiftly—as if she is even expecting their arrival.

When the king summons Rahab and says, "Bring me the spies who are hiding in your home!" Rahab doesn't even flinch. She tells the king they are long gone and quickly hides them—under the flax on her roof.

Rahab is a woman with a plan.

How else can she act so quickly? No, I'm not saying she *knew* the spies would come to her home. But she is watching and expecting God to move. She has already made up her mind. She will follow.

As the spies are hiding on the roof, Rahab declares her fear of God. She knows of the parting of the Red Sea and the defeat of Israel's enemies—and that all of Jericho is trembling. She proclaims, "The LORD your God is he who is God in heaven above and on earth beneath."[2]

In other words, Rahab is already trusting God even before she knows him. Her trust is real, and her readiness shows her preparation. Rahab prepares herself physically, mentally, and spiritually. The roof is predesignated as a clever hiding place. The decision is made—she will protect the spies at all cost. She will leave behind her home and possessions. She will betray her own people. She will save her family, but only if they are willing. And she will serve a God she doesn't yet know.

Don't think she made all of these decisions in a matter of moments. Rahab spent many evenings, perhaps many sleepless nights, getting herself ready. She knew that a window of opportunity would open. She just didn't know where, when, or how.

Rahab's readiness catches me by surprise. Maybe because it's so unusual.

If God acted swiftly and powerfully in my life right now, would I even be ready?

No Risk, No Reward

Not only does Rahab jump. She jumps hard. She jumps high. She decides to risk everything. The king knows the spies entered her home. He is counting on her loyalty to capture these strangers. He needs her to eliminate the threat of invasion. Yet she betrays him, knowing the price of treason is likely her life.

Rahab doesn't just risk her relationship with the king. She risks the safety of her entire family. Even if she doesn't get caught, who says the spies will help her? Will they even spare her life? What business does she have trusting two strangers for her future, let alone the future of her family?

Rahab risks everything *before* the spies cut her a deal. It's *after* she hides them and betrays the king that she begs them to spare both her and her family.

> "Now then, please swear to me by the LORD that, as I have dealt kindly with you, you also will deal kindly with my father's house, and give me a sure sign that you will save alive my father and mother,

my brothers and sisters, and all who belong to
them, and deliver our lives from death."[3]

Rahab's actions speak louder than her words. She first puts her
trust in God. Not in the spies. Her faith isn't dependent on their
response. Nor is it dependent on circumstances. Too often, we
wait on circumstances before we take a risk. We want everything
to fall into place just perfectly. And we want to see all the cards
before we play our hands. But not Rahab. She plays her trump
card and bets everything, well before she cuts a deal.

Rahab's risk pays off. The spies promise to spare Rahab and
her family so long as she keeps their secret. She is instructed
to place a scarlet cord outside her window so that the Israelites
know to spare everyone in her home during the battle of Jericho.
Rahab secretly lowers the spies out her window and waits for
their return. Next time, the spies will come in battle.

Does she wait in fear or anticipation? Probably both. Does
her family question her authority when she commands them
to gather in her home and lock the door? Do they think she is
crazy? Yes. And yes.

This kind of risk is almost unheard of, especially among
women. Too often, we feel trapped by circumstances and family
obligations. We desperately want to trust God for a sea change,
but there is too much at stake. What if our plans backfire? Too
many people are counting on us. Who will take care of the future
if we don't take care of it ourselves?

Rahab likely has these same questions. Yet the great irony is
this—in risking her life, she gains the life she has always longed
for. It's a classic case of no risk, no reward.

Moving beyond Regret

Rahab's story doesn't stop when she escapes Jericho. She goes on to make a new life for herself and her family—to live among the people of Israel. To adopt their customs, make friends with their people, and serve their God. And from what we can tell, Rahab doesn't look back.

Again, Rahab doesn't allow the past to define her. I'm sure many still referred to her as "Rahab the prostitute." When the Bible references Rahab, she's usually referred to as "Rahab the prostitute" or "Rahab the harlot." Even *after* she leaves her life of prostitution, the New Testament refers to her repeatedly as a "prostitute" or "harlot."[4]

Yet she doesn't allow a label to hold her down.

Letting go of the past is never easy. Every time Rahab hears the word *prostitute* she probably wants to crawl out of her skin. She likely sticks out among the Israelites like a sore thumb. As a foreigner in a new culture, she doesn't have a husband to protect her. And it's not like her family is of any assistance. She probably has to tell them to cut out the Jericho "potty talk" around the Israelites. *Would you please stop taking God's name in vain? It's hard enough for us to blend in around here, and you're making things more difficult!*

Not only does Rahab talk and act differently, she looks different. She is probably dark skinned. Any respectable Israelite would consider her unclean. Prostitutes are stoned under the law, and she is lucky to be alive. I can just hear the women of Israel gossiping. "Why did the spies enter the home of a harlot in the first place? What else did she do to get them to cut a deal?" These women will never accept Rahab. And she knows it.

Under these circumstances, most of us would become obsessed with the weight of the past. Not Rahab. She holds her head high. She doesn't look back. She wins the trust and respect of the people. And God gives us all a surprise ending.

Is God Really This Amazing?

Here is where the story gets even better. Rahab stars as the leading lady in *Pretty Woman*. She doesn't just leave her past behind, she rides into the sunset on a white horse with a prince. She becomes a bride.

Rahab marries a man named Salmon, none other than the son of Judah's tribal leader. In other words, she doesn't just marry, she marries well! She has a son named Boaz, and from Boaz's descendants King David, the greatest king in all of Israel, will rise. And from the line of David comes the fruit of Eve's seed—Jesus Christ, the Messiah.

Just think, from Eve's screwup to Rahab the prostitute, God delights in giving women second chances for greatness. Not just second chances to escape—second chances to be center stage as part of his plan. Rahab takes her place in history as one of five women mentioned in the lineage of Christ.[5] She is one of two women mentioned in the faith hall of fame.[6] Not bad for a Jericho prostitute!

Clearly, Rahab doesn't set out to be a matriarch. She is just trying to get out of a lousy job. Yet God wants to give her so much more. A woman who once had a barren tummy and an inn full of drunken men now has a hope, a future, and a place in history. I don't think Rahab ever imagined in her wildest dreams that she would bear the progenitors of the Messiah. Yet God shows us that he is able do more than we ever could ask or imagine.

James tells us that Rahab was justified by her faith. "In the same way, was not even Rahab the prostitute considered righteous for what she did when she gave lodging to the spies and sent them off in a different direction?"[7]

When I reread this verse, it dawns on me. Rahab is still a prostitute when God uses her. She hasn't yet left her old life. She doesn't yet know the God of Israel. Yet he still credits her faith as righteousness. It's not about who she is or where she's been, it's about who God is and where he is taking her.

A God of Second Chances

Rahab speaks to women today in all walks of life. Women who are overworked and undervalued, women who are trapped in a cycle of oppression and sin, women who need a way out but don't have a mentor to follow.

I look at the barmaid sitting in the corner. I see the way the owner looks at her, and I know she probably gives him more than a full day's work. Her eyes tell me she is trapped, and I know instinctively that she longs for something more.

I see my friend Kate struggling to make ends meet. She's tempted to use her sexuality to gain an advantage at work, and she's probably crossed the line with her boss. She too wants out but doesn't know where to go next.

I talk to my neighbor who works long, hard hours. She wants to make a change, but she is afraid of the future. She's a single mom, and she just can't afford to take the risk.

Many of us are more like Rahab than we care to admit. Often, we think everything has to line up before we step out in faith. Yet, like Rahab, God can use our *present* work for something more. Sure, Rahab's inn is a den of sin, but it is also a haven for the spies. Her relationship with the king is unseemly, but God uses it to distract Israel's pursuers. The location of Rahab's home is a magnet for prostitution, but it is also a window of escape. Like so many of us, Rahab's work isn't all good or all bad. And God doesn't wait for her circumstances to change before he calls her to act. Then, God blesses her beyond her wildest dreams.

How many times have we prayed to God, "Just get me out!"

Yet God is looking to do so much more. If I listen closely, I can hear him answer, "I'm not only going to get you out. I'm going to get you in!"

Discussion Questions for Chapter Two

1. Can you relate to the multiple hats worn by Rahab? Which hat do you most relate to?

2. Have you ever felt stuck in a job or trapped by circumstances? If so, what was your response? What can you learn from Rahab?

3. Read Ephesians 3:20. What does this verse mean to a woman who is just trying to survive? What impact does it make to know that God wants to give us so much more?

4. Do you know a woman who needs a second chance? If so, commit to share Rahab's story with her.

ঌ *Select readings:* Joshua chapters 2 and 6

Chapter Two Notes

1. Virginia Stem Owens, *Daughters of Eve: Women of the Bible Speak to Women Today* (Colorado Springs, CO: Navpress, 1995) gives a nice overview of Rahab's plight as well as some welcome historical context for our discussion.
2. Joshua 2:11 (RSV).
3. Joshua 2:12–13 (ESV).
4. Hebrews 11:31; James 2:25.
5. Matthew 1: 1–17.
6. Hebrews 11.
7. James 2:25.

Chapter Three

DEBORAH
A Time to Lead

Deborah wears more hats than just about any other woman I know. She's a mother, wife, counselor, judge, deliverer, spiritual and political leader, and prophetess. If she lived today, she'd have her own hit reality TV show. She's a combination of *Judge Judy, The Good Wife,* and *Undercover Boss* all wrapped into one.

Deborah knows what's it's like to sit in the boardroom and make tough decisions. And not only is she in the boardroom, she's at the head of the table. She calls the shots. She's the kind of woman who takes on more and more responsibility because she knows how to get things done. And she's not power hungry. Just the opposite. She'd rather delegate, but she's also not afraid to get her hands dirty when duty calls.

I really want to be like Deborah.

STARTING WITH HUMBLE ROOTS

Let's back up a minute. I know what you're thinking. *I'm not like Deborah! I'm never going to be a judge or lead a nation. She's just too far out of reach for me to understand let alone relate to.*

I get it. So before we start to feel completely and totally inadequate, let's remember that leadership takes time. Deborah wasn't always in charge. It's not like she became famous overnight. Like most leaders, she is tried and tested. God prepares and trains Deborah for years and years. And her humble roots reveal much about her character.

Deborah is the wife of an obscure man named Lapidoth. He is largely an unknown figure. In other words, Deborah doesn't rise to power through marriage. And she appears to be both a wife and mother. Importantly, Deborah is both a wife *and* a mother. And while Scripture doesn't tell us about her children, we can imagine that being a devoted homemaker—in addition to everything else on her plate—is central to her life.

So how does Deborah go from being a wife and mother to leading the nation of Israel? Like many leaders, Deborah is faithful in what God gives her. And she starts at home.

Deborah shows that we don't need to have a prestigious career, get a second degree, or become politically and socially connected. More often than not, God wants to start by using us in our own backyards. In Deborah's case, it was her *front* yard.

SETTING UP SHOP IN THE FRONT YARD

Deborah lives on a road between Ramah and Bethel in the "hill country" of Ephraim.[1] In other words, she lives out in the middle of nowhere. She's not a city girl by birth, and she's not part of the "in" crowd in Jerusalem. Yet God strategically places her home on a traveled path where visitors come and seek her counsel. It is under a royal palm tree, probably in her front yard, where Deborah starts in business. Her first job outside the home and temple is that of a counselor. She can't afford a cushy office space. The great thing about the front yard? The rent is free.

I like to think of her as the classic work-at-home mom. The kids are running around the house, she puts down her newborn for a nap, and during her afternoon "break," when she's supposed to finish laundry and get dinner started, she has a line of people waiting under the palm tree for her counsel.

Talk about a woman in demand.

Importantly, Deborah will later serve in battle. Yet she trains at a time of peace, at home. There is something about this training that keeps her grounded. Her reputation spreads far and wide. She proves to be faithful in wise counsel, and God provides her with more responsibility.

I can just hear Deborah as she starts to feel pulled in too many directions.

Lord, I have so much on my plate right now. I'm busy with the kids and our home, but the people keep coming and coming to see me. I can't turn them away. I don't want to turn them away. You're just going to have to guide and direct me.

DEBORAH GETS A PROMOTION

Like most capable women who have too much to do, Deborah keeps taking on more. And more. Her hard work pays off. Not only is she recognized as a counselor to the people, she next becomes a judge and ruler. While Deborah likely starts with personal and domestic counsel, she is now entrusted with solving disputes of the law and governing the people. And she isn't just God's choice. She's the people's choice. Deborah is the only woman in the Bible who is put in political power at the consent of the people.

Think about it. Deborah wins the people's choice award. She doesn't take over by force or might. Like Huldah (who we'll study in Chapter Six), her reputation as a trusted counselor and spiritual leader draws people to her. She doesn't seek power, yet God gives her power.

Meet Judge Deborah.

I don't know Deborah's age when she becomes judge. But I tend to believe she has a few grey hairs—and that it is a promotion long overdue. There's just no evidence that Deborah is thrust into power unprepared. Nor is there evidence that she pushes others out to get ahead. Instead, Deborah is patient, trained, and ready.

Deborah advocates for the people. She burns with indignation at injustice and oppression. She's not afraid to take action. She tells a business owner when he needs to pay his workers a fair wage. She punishes a young man for taking advantage of a young woman. She forgives a widow in debt, but then she orders the family to make restitution. She runs her courtroom with a velvet glove. And the people listen.

Deborah's influence extends far outside her courtroom. Does Deborah view the people as powerless against outside force? Hardly. Instead, she exhorts the people to rise up against their oppressors. To conquer fear and complacency. And she doesn't just tell them to revolt for the sake of a fight. She seeks and hears from God.

Lord, I'm so grateful for this privilege. But I'm also really scared. I'm the only woman to serve as a judge. Are you sure you want me to continue? Some of the men don't respect me, and my work has put a strain on my family and my relationship with Lapidoth. Yet if you continue to lead me, I will lead the people.

Do I Have to Become a Warrior, God?

It would have been easy for Deborah to keep giving orders from the bench. After all, she's good at it. She has a platform. She has followers. No one expects her to enter the battlefield. Isn't carrying out a war somebody else's job?

Here's where Deborah sets herself apart. She's already broken every stereotype in biblical history. Now she does the unthinkable. She doesn't just give the men orders to fight. She leads them in battle. What is she thinking?

Call me crazy, but how many little girls say, "Mom, I want to be a warrior when I grow up." Not me. Don't you think Deborah would have rather sent the men to battle alone? Of course. I think she would have rather stayed under the palm tree and told her husband, "Hey, honey—can you go lead the army in battle today? I have some laundry to do."

Talk is cheap. Anyone can give an order, but it's another thing to actually get it done. Deborah puts her money where her mouth is and accompanies the army to fight. Don't think she makes this decision lightly. Deborah doesn't want war any more than you or I. Yet she is so confident in God's deliverance of the people that she both orders and leads the army.

Deborah gives a new meaning to putting your neck on the line.

At this point on the journey, I'd say to God, "This isn't what I signed up for. The palm tree thing was fun. The judge gig wasn't bad either. But you've got to be kidding me. Please tell me I am hallucinating. Battle? Me?"

A WOMAN ON A MISSION

Deborah shows us what God can do with a fiery spirit and a little faith. With determination in her eyes and fire in her belly, she summons one of Israel's military leaders, Barak, from his home town. Deborah puts a team together. She delegates. She knows she can't do it alone, and she knows Barak's strengths as well as his weaknesses. He has the skill, but he doesn't have the stomach. They work out a military plan together. Barak is shaking in his boots. While he trusts Deborah's judgment, he doesn't share her confidence. Simply put, he is scared to death. Deborah tries to reassure him. She tells him, "Go," clearly taking authority. She doesn't give him a choice, she gives him an order. But it's no use. He wants her to go with him.

Barak says to her, "If you go with me, I will go; but if you don't go with me, I won't go."[2]

Most of us would have walked away. If Barak lacks this much confidence, it is time to turn back. Besides, what if Barak gets into battle and decides to chicken out? Then, who will be left holding the bag?

Look Lord, you know I'm willing to do anything for you. But I didn't sign up for this. I'm a wife and a mother. I'm not trained in battle. Even if I can lead Barak to water, how am I supposed to make him drink? Isn't this is asking a bit much?

Yet this isn't Deborah's response. If she has any hesitation, she doesn't show it. She maintains her cool. After all, Barak is already freaked out, so she knows she has to hold it together—at least on the outside. And I don't believe Deborah's strength is an act. Deborah knows it's not about her. And she knows it's not up to her.

DEBORAH THE PROPHET

Deborah doesn't just judge, lead, and win in battle. She speaks the truth about the future—acting as both a leader and a prophet. Her response to Barak's fears? She tells it like it is. She will go with him, but the Lord will deliver, not her. And Barak won't get any glory. "'Very well,' Deborah said, 'I will go with you. But because of the way you are going about this, the honor will not be yours, for the LORD will hand Sisera over to a woman.'"[3]

Deborah knows that Israel isn't riding on her shoulders, it's riding on God's shoulders. So she assures Barak with confidence that God will deliver. Deborah further predicts that a woman will slay the enemy. (If you care to read the story of Jael, you'll learn she's one brave woman who stabs the leader of the enemy in her tent!)[4]

Deborah's prophecy comes true. God delivers Israel in battle—with Deborah at Barak's side—and the land has rest for forty years.

That's right, forty years of peace. Quite a reign for a work-at-home mom who set up shop in the front yard.

START SMALL, THINK BIG

Deborah's extraordinary leadership boils down to a few key points. Start small. Be faithful. Be willing to go big or go home. It's a winning strategy for any leader in training.

Like Deborah, there are leaders in the making all around us. Most female leaders fall into two categories: (1) women who don't want to start small or (2) women who don't want to go big. Most of us are some combination.

What do I mean by women who don't want to start small? I can speak here from experience. I tend to live for pipe dreams. I set unrealistic expectations and make grand plans. I also overlook small victories and expect God to act "big" or not act at all. Yet more often than not, God wants to start small. He wants us to be faithful with the little things first—even if we think we are capable of more "important" work. Yet God doesn't need us to rent expensive office space or appear on stage, he just needs us to step out in our front yards.

Women who don't want to go big have the opposite problem. They sit on a gold mine, yet don't want to dig. Leadership is somebody else's job. They're too afraid to fail, they struggle with lack of "qualifications," or they don't want to get their hands dirty. Besides, it's so comfortable in the backyard. Why step into the front yard (or worse, center stage) when things are fine just the way they are?

Deborah models leadership to both kinds of women. She starts small and grows her reputation from humble roots. Yet she isn't afraid to go big. She knows she's not in the fight alone. With God on her side, she need not fear the spotlight.

GOD IS AHEAD OF OUR TIME

Deborah is ahead of her time by more than a few centuries. It's completely unheard of for a woman to command political, social, and spiritual authority in biblical history. She's the exception, not the norm. Does this mean that God prefers using men? That God will only use a woman when he can't find a man for the job?

I've heard some scholars downplay Deborah's leadership as an anomaly. It's not uncommon to hear statements like, "Well, none of the men would step up, so God *had* to use a woman." When I read Deborah's story, I'm just not buying it.

Let's face it. God could have used a man to deliver Israel. He didn't. He uses Deborah because of who she is, not in spite of who she is. This shows us that God isn't limited by circumstance, culture, or even gender. Simply put, God is ahead of our time.

God makes an incredible statement when he appoints a wife and mother as CEO, senator, and spiritual leader. I think God had a big grin on his face watching Deborah lead the men into battle, cheering her on every step of the way. Certainly, there were critics in Deborah's time who didn't think she could do it. But God did it anyway.

Could it be that God raises up Deborah because he knows just how much we need her leadership *today*?

Discussion Questions for Chapter Three

1. Do you think Deborah set out to be a judge? By starting small, how does she build her credibility as a leader?

2. The Bible doesn't speak of Deborah's critics. Yet, given her unprecedented leadership, we can imagine resistance to her authority. How do you think Deborah dealt with her critics?

3. Has God ever asked you to put your neck on the line? If so, how did you respond? What can you learn from Deborah?

4. Do you agree that women in leadership either don't want to start small or don't want to go big? Which barrier do you most relate to?

&❧ *Select readings:* Judges chapter 4

Chapter Three Notes

1. Judges 4:5.
2. Judges 4:8.
3. Judges 4:9.
4. While we won't cover Jael in any detail, the rest of her story appears in Judges chapter 4.

Chapter Four

RUTH
Embracing Plan C

'm a big fan of Julia Roberts, but something about the movie *Eat, Pray, Love* didn't resonate with me. Maybe because I had been reading about Ruth. I couldn't help but think, *How would this story change if Ruth played the leading role? What if Ruth stormed Hollywood?*

The lead character, Liz Gilbert (played by Julia Roberts) sets out on a journey to find herself. Liz and Ruth couldn't be more different.

- While Liz sets out to find herself, Ruth sets out to lose herself.
- Liz is in a bad situation. She gets out. Ruth is in a worse situation. She stays in.
- Liz jumps in bed with a new man. Ruth goes to bed alone.
- Liz heads to a foreign land to indulge. Ruth heads to a foreign land to sacrifice.

- Liz tells God she will find her own way. Ruth tells Naomi, "Your people will be my people and your God my God."[1]

Ruth would never make it in Hollywood.

TIME FOR A CHANGE IN HOLLYWOOD?

Ruth defies our modern-day notions about freedom and relationships. Rather than abandoning a relationship to find herself, she makes a costly commitment. It's one thing to lose yourself for a man. But Ruth loses herself for an older women—her mother-in-law!

Ruth isn't going to win an Oscar for her performance. Not that she isn't beautiful, passionate, and engaging. We just can't relate to her devotion. We like to see ourselves in Hollywood, and most of us are more like Liz.

Liz tells her husband, "I don't want to be in this marriage." She stews. She whines. She gets out. Isn't that what we do when we're stuck in a bad situation? We beg God to release us. How many times have we said to God, "I don't want to be in this house," "I don't want to be in this job," or even, "I don't want to be in this marriage?"

Yet Ruth shows us the power of old-fashioned commitment and self-sacrifice. It's high time for Ruth to storm Hollywood.

Ruth's story has been told and retold for centuries. She's one of two women in the Bible to have an entire book named after her. Countless Bible studies have been written about her. Frankly, we can't do her justice in a single chapter. So we won't cover everything. We're not going to cover the classic love story between Ruth and Boaz in any detail. Nor will we cover the compelling allegory of redemption and grace that extends between God and his people from generation to generation.

Here's what we're going to do instead. We're going to take a close look at Ruth's work—a piece of her story that is often overlooked. Ruth's work involves patience, forbearance, and some serious elbow grease. Simply put, Ruth isn't afraid of a hard day's work.

WHEN THE DECK IS STACKED AGAINST YOU

Before we dig into Ruth's work, let's set the scene. Ruth is a young Moabite living sometime between 1000 and 1400 BC. She marries into a Jewish family who had relocated to Moab during a famine, looking for a better life. And as luck would have it, Ruth's husband dies. So she's stuck with an old mother-in-law, Naomi, and a sister-in-law, Orpah (also a widow). Naomi's husband is also dead—not a particularly strong line of men in the family.

So Ruth, Orpah, and Naomi are alone. They must fend for themselves.

Naomi determines she will leave Moab and head back to Israel. Ruth and Orpah insist on coming with her. Orpah makes it half way—probably to the border. But Naomi urges both her and Ruth to turn back. To make a new life. To find new husbands. Orpah reluctantly heads back to Moab. But not Ruth. She is too stubborn. She won't leave Naomi and she proclaims that she will follow Naomi's God.

It's not like Ruth doesn't have other options. She is probably a spring chicken. She is unattached. She can start over and "find herself" if she wants to.

Instead, she embarks on a 120-mile journey with an old woman to a foreign land. She must count the cost. She could be homeless. A widow forever. An outcast among the Jews. She would be hated as a Moabite. I hope she was savvy enough to leave her Moabite headdress behind since her language and complexion would draw enough attention. The odds are stacked against her. Better to find yourself in Moab than lose yourself in a foreign land. Yet for reasons I don't completely understand, instead of finding herself in Moab, Ruth chooses to lose herself in Israel. She embraces Plan C.

EMBRACING PLAN C

Ruth isn't the first young woman to face disappointment. Most young women have dreams, get married, and hope for children. Some women put their dreams in education and career progression—hoping to land their dream job and become financially secure before having a family (or at least before wrinkles set in). Yet, more often than not, things don't go as planned.

Ruth has these same hopes and dreams. She wants a family, stability, and personal fulfillment. As a woman living in ancient Moab, Ruth is fully dependent on her husband for support. But he dies young. Before giving Ruth any children. That was Plan A.

On to Plan B. Find another man. Dump Naomi. Get on with your life.

Plan B isn't just the obvious choice. It appears to be the only choice. There is no other logical solution. Forget fairy tales and romance, Ruth needs a provider. She needs offspring. She needs a future. Any woman in Ruth's shoes would opt for Plan B.

But not Ruth. Instead, she does the illogical. She becomes a provider. She takes on a burden. She sets out to support herself and her mother-in-law. Heck, Ruth doesn't just refuse Plan B, she invents Plan C. Leave your homeland, take on the burden of an aging mother-in-law, and move to a new country where you will be an outcast and discriminated against. There is no playbook for Plan C.

WHEN THERE'S NO UNEMPLOYMENT TO DRAW

It's not like Ruth can say to Naomi, "Don't worry, we'll just live off of unemployment until we get on our feet." Or, "I'll take out some loans, go to college, and eventually get a good job."

No, Ruth's choice is to be destitute and likely homeless. Short of prostitution, it's not like a single woman had means to earn a living. And don't think it didn't enter their minds. Surely, Naomi worried that Ruth would end up on the streets in order to support both of them.

Understandably, Naomi tries to dissuade her. They have no way to make a living. No men to rely on. She knows Ruth will be an outsider—maybe even an outcast in Israel. And Naomi isn't exactly full of sunshine. The glass is more than half empty. She doesn't say, "I can't wait to get home. God will provide for a safe journey." She doesn't encourage Ruth that the future will be better for either of them. No, she's broken and beaten down. She's changed her name to Mara, meaning "bitter." And she lets everyone know it. Including Ruth.

Why doesn't Ruth look for a way out? Notwithstanding that there is no unemployment to draw, she is either incredibly faithful or incredibly stubborn. Or both. She gives us all a lesson in work.

Do the work that is given to you. Work hard. Keep your options open.

DOING THE WORK THAT IS GIVEN

Ruth and Naomi learn that the famine in Judah had broken. Ruth is paying close attention. She sees how it works. She can go out to the fields and pick up stalks of grain left behind by the harvesters. A process called "gleaning"—reserved for the poor and widows—is a means to support both Ruth and Naomi. At least for the short term.

Note that Ruth isn't given a handout. She doesn't ask for one. She is prepared to work.

It's not her dream job. As far as she knows, it's a dead end. She could be stuck gleaning for the rest of her life—if she is lucky. Harvesters are a rough bunch. What if the harvesters try to take advantage of Ruth? What's a young, foreign woman to do in the fields without a protector?

Ruth could have told God, "Hey, you must have made a mistake here. I'm meant to do something much more important. What about my resume?"

She is overqualified to be a gleaner. It is beneath her! Yet God hasn't forgotten about her. He just calls her to first do the work in front of her. No complaining. No grumbling. Just do your work.

Many of us can relate to Ruth. We don't want to do the work that God has given us. We think God has forgotten completely about our resumes—our skill sets, our unique qualifications to do something else. Something more important.

Even the Apostle Paul—arguably the most effective New Testament leader—likely had these same thoughts. Look how he first responds when God tells him he will be sent away to the Gentiles.[2]

> God: "Leave Jerusalem immediately, because the people here will not accept your testimony about me."
>
> Paul: "These people know that I went from one synagogue to another to imprison and beat those who believe in you. And when the blood of your martyr Stephen was shed, I stood there giving my approval and guarding the clothes of those who were killing him."

Paul is probably thinking to himself: *Wait a minute, I'm uniquely cut out to work in Jerusalem, remember? After all, I have been an insider. I know the ropes. I understand the culture. I have even walked in the shoes of those who persecute Christians. I can make a difference right here! I'm the guy to do it.*

God's response? "Go; I will send you far away to the Gentiles."[3]

Did God forget about Paul's resume? After all, why would God send a highly qualified insider out of his home territory to a place where he has nothing in common with the culture, geography, or religion of the people?

It's like sending a young Moabite to Israel to glean after the harvest.

WORKING TOO HARD FOR A LIVING?

All of the women we have studied thus far—Eve, Rahab, and Deborah—work hard for a living. Some would say *too* hard. Many of us can relate. And we can't help but notice this repeated theme—women who work hard tend to get things done!

Likewise, Ruth doesn't just work. She works her tail off. It's one thing to faithfully show up for work. It's another thing to do a good job. Gleaning is *really* miserable work. Working from dawn till dusk. Bending over in the hot sun. Relying on the scraps of others.

Yet Ruth lives out the New Testament command of good work: "We are God's workmanship, created in Christ Jesus to do good works, which God prepared in advance for us to do."[4] In other words, we are supposed to do more than go through the motions. This means pursuing excellence. Getting to work on time. Maintaining a good attitude. In fact, God even prepares our good work in advance. The Greek word for "workmanship" is actually *poiema*. It's where we get the English word *poem*, and it is often used in Scripture to refer to God's creative activity.

I see Ruth as living out her work as a poem. With every stalk of grain she gleans, she allows God to do his creative work in and through her. Don't think she is just picking up grain, she is allowing God to write his words on her heart, mind, and soul so that she can give the performance of a lifetime.

And what a performance. Ruth's work is noticed.

WHEN HARD WORK EARNS FAVOR

The foreman reports to Boaz, the owner of the field, that Ruth has an unquestionable work ethic. She works hard all morning and only stops once to rest in the shade. Ruth isn't the kind of worker who milks her sick days, takes advantage of the boss, or nods off on the job when nobody's looking.

Her hard work earns her favor. Boaz tells her to stay in his field and stay close to the servant girls. He promises that the men won't bother her. He gives her water and an extra portion of food. He even instructs the men to leave her extra grain.

Boaz hasn't just noticed Ruth—he has noticed her work.

He tells Ruth, "May the LORD reward your work."[5]

He doesn't say, *May the LORD reward your devotion*, or *may the LORD reward your beauty*, or *may the LORD reward your talent*.

Ruth is rewarded for her work!

Isn't it interesting that Ruth's work is the first thing that catches Boaz's eye? As women, too often we rely on beauty and talent to earn favor, especially with men. Yet Boaz's response to Ruth shows us how hard work sets us apart.

WHEN THE BOSS GIVES GRACE

Some of us can relate more to Boaz than Ruth. We're in charge of our own "vineyard." Maybe it's small, but we have influence over the people who work for or around us. And we can benefit from Boaz's approach to work.

Boaz starts by using his position and resources to extend common grace to Ruth. I view common grace as simply extending kindness because it's the right thing to do—not expecting anything in return. Boaz uses his position to be kind to a foreigner. In showing compassion to a poor widow, he doesn't expect that she will become his wife. While the story of Ruth and Boaz may end with a wedding, it starts with Boaz extending common grace to a stranger for her good work.[6]

Ruth doesn't abuse this grace or take it for granted. Nor does she stop working hard. Once Ruth finds favor with Boaz (and she learns from Naomi that Boaz is a distant relative), she could have immediately requested a promotion. She could have said, "My sugar daddy has arrived. No more gleaning for me!"

But she doesn't.

When I first heard the story of Ruth, I assumed that she gleaned for a week at most, before being noticed by Boaz. But this is not the case. Ruth clearly works *through the harvest.* She doesn't quit. While Ruth has every right to ask for the "friends and family" plan, she never asks for special treatment. Even after Ruth knows Boaz has noticed her, she continues to work hard. Maybe harder than ever.

KEEP YOUR OPTIONS OPEN

Like Rahab, Ruth isn't stuck in the past. She doesn't want to be a gleaner forever any more than you or I want to be stuck in a dead-end job. And she's not afraid to hope for something more.

Nor is Ruth completely naïve. She knows she has found favor with Boaz. She knows he's the owner of the vineyard, and she knows he's related to Naomi.

At some point, the light bulb switched on. *Boaz can provide more than a field to glean in. He is unattached and available.*

At what point does she connect the dots? We don't know for sure. But notice that Ruth is paying attention—she is keeping her options open. With open hands and a broken heart, Ruth is ready for redemption.

Ruth could have easily missed the path of redemption. She could have continued gleaning. Working hard. With her head down. After all, she was getting by. She and Naomi weren't starving. Why should she expect more? Why should she ask for more?

Some of us believe we should be gleaners forever. We don't believe there is anything more. We don't hope, and we certainly don't ask God for redemption. We're too scared. Or maybe we're clueless. Sometimes, when we're gleaning, we don't even look up. It's just easier to work with your head down.

If Ruth refuses (or forgets) to look up, she will miss it. She won't see God's provision right in front of her if she's too busy working. She won't see that God wants to do something bigger and better with her work.

But Ruth is alert. She shows us the balance between finishing the job and reaching for something more. She shows us there is a time to be content with the status quo. To work hard and finish the harvest. But there is also a time to take notice. To look up. To keep doors open. To ask to be more than a gleaner.

Too Old to Make a Difference?

Enter Naomi. What can an old worn-down woman contribute at this late stage in life? We already know she is bitter. She's past retirement and she must rely on others to care for her. Her ship has sailed and her work is over.

Or is it?

We can't underestimate Naomi's influence in this process. Without Naomi, Ruth might still be gleaning. To the extent Ruth is initially unaware of God's provision, Naomi doesn't miss a beat. She is looking to the next harvest and the harvest thereafter. And she's several steps ahead of Ruth.

Let's not miss Naomi's work.

Naomi doesn't sit on her hands. She isn't passive, and she doesn't simply hope for the best and prepare for the worst. No. She takes action. She too works.

Naomi is too old to work in the fields, but she does have a few resources of her own. Namely, she has two things: land and influence.

She uses both.

Understand, she too takes risk. The land provides some security—even a last resort. Maybe it's her retirement plan. She doesn't hang onto her land to see if the market turns. She puts it on the table, knowing that a relative closer than Boaz has the right of first refusal. What if he actually buys it? What if he is a jerk? He could ruin everything. By Jewish law, whoever buys the land will also have to marry Ruth—it is a package deal. Who will come to the rescue of a Moabite widow? For all we know, it is illegal in those days to marry a Moabite. It certainly isn't encouraged. Whoever buys the land can mistreat Ruth and probably get away with it.

Yet Naomi puts her only piece of security—land—on the line. She works by using the resources she has.

Naomi's influence is her second recourse. Influence isn't something that is given; it is something that is earned. It has taken her years and years to build this influence over Ruth, and

Naomi knows how to use it. She may be old, but she's still got a few tricks up her sleeve. She tells Ruth to approach Boaz late at night on the threshing floor. I happen to think Boaz is one of those guys who needs more than a nudge to know that a woman is interested in him.

So with Naomi as the "matchmaker," Ruth listens. She acts. She's willing to put her trust in an old woman—a woman who isn't perfect but who has her best interest at heart. She's willing to bet that God uses other people—often older mentors—to get our attention when we're busy gleaning.

Ruth presents herself to Boaz. She sits at his feet in anticipation. But she must wait.

The ball is in Boaz's court.

More Than a Happy Ending

Boaz wants to marry Ruth. While others may see her foreign blood as tainted and unattractive, Boaz understands all too well. After all, he is the grandson of none other than Rahab! He too has some foreign blood in his veins. Maybe that's why he's still single after all these years. He doesn't exactly have a "proper" blood line. Maybe he sees the women in his own family mistreated or discriminated against because of Rahab. This makes him the compassionate man he is and further draws him to Ruth.

He wants to buy the field. But he can't. Another man—a nearer relative—has the right of first refusal. So he heads to town and confronts the man head-on. He takes witnesses. And when the man declines the purchase (probably because of Ruth), Boaz acts quickly. Like his grandmother Rahab, he is decisive when it counts. He steps in and buys the land. He takes Ruth as his bride, and the rest is history.

Because of the good work of Ruth, Naomi, and Boaz, King David is born two generations later. And Ruth makes her way into the genealogy of Jesus Christ. It's so much more than a happy ending. And it's just like God to turn hard work into redemption—something more than Ruth could have hoped or imagined.

Discussion Questions for Chapter Four

1. Do you struggle doing work that is "beneath" you or seems unimportant? Have you felt that God has forgotten about your resume?

2. Notice how Ruth gives up everything yet gains even more. Read Matthew 16:25. How does this verse apply to Ruth?

3. How do we respond when Plan A falls apart? Have you ever embraced Plan C?

4. Can you relate most to the work of Ruth, Boaz, or Naomi? Notice how God uses each of us in different ways to accomplish his plan.

&* *Select readings:* The book of Ruth

CHAPTER FOUR NOTES

1. Ruth 1:16.
2. See Acts chapter 22.
3. Acts 22:21.
4. Ephesians 2:10.
5. Ruth 2:12 (NASB).
6. For a compelling discussion of the common grace in the story of Ruth and Boaz, see Tom Nelson, *Work Matters* (Wheaton, IL: Crossway, 2011), 131–32.

Chapter Five

JEZEBEL
The Ultimate Power Trip

Most of us like happy endings. We long to see good overcome evil, and we embrace stories about redemption and second chances. We celebrate women like Rahab and Ruth who aren't afraid to become humble and broken, and we love when God picks up the broken pieces of our humanity and puts us back together.

Queen Jezebel is neither humble nor broken. And nothing about her story is good. This is the only chapter in this book that doesn't give us a happy ending.

So why are we wasting our time? If nothing about her story is good, why not skip Jezebel completely and move on?

I gave this serious consideration. But, like it or not, we live in a broken world. And evil often prevails in our work. If we're going to study the working women of the Bible, it's tough to leave Jezebel off the table. She is one of the most powerful women in biblical history. She is both a political and religious leader. She commands authority. She exerts serious influence over her husband. She knows how to get things done. Besides, sometimes we have to witness the dark side of life so that we run to the light.

Jezebel also teaches us that evil does not discriminate. Nor is evil based on gender. Women are just as capable of evil as men. Sure, I realize that most of the wars in this world have been started and fought by men, most violent acts are committed by men, and most convicted criminals are men. But testosterone is not a prerequisite for evil. And just because women are historically less violent than men, we should never discount the potential for evil in our lives. Evil can utterly destroy our souls and in the process destroy anything and everything around us. In Jezebel's case, evil is an all-consuming fire that must be quenched.

Not the Poster Child for Sunday School

I'm guessing that most of you didn't study Jezebel in Sunday school. Me neither. Maybe you've never even heard of her. A loose woman or prostitute is sometimes referred to as a "Jezebel," but Queen Jezebel is otherwise ignored by most of us. You can read more about her in the books of the Kings.[1] At best, we take her name in vain. She's just not Sunday school material.

Lord Acton's famous line sums up Jezebel well. "Power corrupts. Absolute power corrupts absolutely."

Such is the story of Jezebel. Here's a short but necessary overview of her reign.[2]

A daughter of a king, Jezebel is born into royalty. Which means she's used to getting what she wants. And she doesn't just want privilege. She wants power. It is said that her father, the priest-king of Tyre, murdered his own brother to become king. Talk about a not-so-positive role model. Jezebel is born into both corruption and evil. So she jumps in with both feet.

Like many ancient women seeking to increase their political influence, Jezebel marries for power. It may have been an arranged marriage, or it may have been her choice. Or both. Either way, it is a match made in hell. Jezebel marries King Ahab of northern Israel, and they quickly become a power couple.

Ahab is just her type. He is both wicked and power hungry. But, more importantly, he doesn't have a backbone, and he's not exactly the sharpest tool in the box. Which means Jezebel walks all over him. She finds him easy to manipulate, and he frankly can't keep up with her. He doesn't even try. It's clear that Jezebel wears the pants in the marriage.

WHEN EVIL TAKES OVER

Jezebel isn't only after political domination. She's after social and spiritual domination. We know that Jezebel's father is a priest of Baal and that Jezebel brings to Israel her own pagan idolatry. Baal, a god of fertility, is worshipped through temple prostitution and even child sacrifice. And Baal's female companion, Astarte, is Jezebel's chosen deity.[3]

What does this mean in practical terms? Jezebel sets up temples of prostitution throughout Israel—where men would "pay" to worship Astarte, and female sex slaves would perform in the name of worship. Given our study of Rahab, this practice isn't surprising in ancient cultures. Not exactly a society that values women.

Jezebel sets up shop in Israel, seeking to permeate the culture with pagan idolatry. And she isn't content to stop there. She wants to eliminate the competition. She utterly and completely loathes the God of Israel, probably because the Jewish laws are completely contrary to all she knows and lives for. And she views Israel's God as a threat to her very existence. So one of her first acts as queen is to order the execution of the prophets of Israel, including King Ahab's nemesis, the prophet Elijah.

GOD SHOWS UP ON THE SCENE

In the midst of Jezebel's reign, God is still at work. And he speaks through the prophet Elijah. Jezebel knows she has to shut him up! But Elijah isn't very easy to catch. He hides out in the wilderness for a couple of years when God strikes the land with a famine. But Jezebel won't give up or take no for an answer. She must eradicate the threat.

When she finally catches up with Elijah, he challenges King Ahab to a duel of the prophets. Ahab agrees to the showdown—either because he is too weak to say no or too desperate to please his wife. At the showdown of Mount Carmel, Elijah summons the prophets of Baal and Astarte to see whether they can command fire from heaven. Of course, they can't. Elijah prepares an altar, and the prophets of Baal can't light a spark. So Elijah decides to rub their noses in failure. (Probably to get a rise out of Jezebel!) He soaks his own altar with water, prays to God, and the people stand by and watch fire from heaven set it ablaze.

God shows up in authority and power. And Jezebel is watching. It's not every day that fire rains down from heaven, even in her world.

How does Jezebel respond to this miracle? Surely, she must be impressed with this divine act. Does she change her evil ways and repent? Hardly. She doesn't even retreat. She pursues Elijah with increased vigor, sending Elijah on the run for several more years. In other words, Jezebel's heart gets even harder. It's at this point that evil completely consumes her like wildfire.

GOING DOWN IN FLAMES

Jezebel continues to wield power over King Ahab. When a common landowner, Nabol, refuses to sell his vineyard to the king, Jezebel takes matters into her own hands and has Nabol falsely accused of blasphemy and treason. She's not the kind of woman who stands around and waits for a man to deliver. She knows that when she wants something done, she has to do it herself. After Nabol is stoned, she proudly presents the field to King Ahab.

See what I mean? Nothing gets in her way.

Several years later, Ahab is murdered, and Jezebel continues to reign as Queen Mother with the help of her sons. After a successful military coup takes place, the captain of the revolting army rides into town to take the queen. Instead of hiding in her room or trying to strike a deal with the new regime, Jezebel is defiant. She goes into her room, fixes her hair, and puts on her best makeup. She taunts the commander out of her window. If she's going to go down, she's going to go down in flames! "Come and get me! You'll have to drag me out of here before I surrender!" The commander Jehu challenges Jezebel's servants to save themselves. So they do. Jezebel's servants throw her out of the window, and her blood spills on the pavement and onto the commander's own horse.

Things don't turn out happily ever after. Jezebel's reign is a recipe for disaster—it's one we don't want to repeat. How does it ever get this bad?

THE RAW MATERIALS ARE THERE

Frankly, Jezebel has the raw materials for effective leadership. She has it all. Talent, courage, and opportunity. Her intelligence is evident by the way she leads and marshals resources. She tells people what to do, and they tend to listen. She knows what she wants and she goes after it. She's not afraid to take a stand. And when failure knocks at her door, she puts on her best outfit and makeup as if to say, "Bring it on!"

Jezebel has the core traits of a modern power woman. And when she enters Israel as the new Queen Bride, she has every opportunity to do good. She wears many hats. She's a wife, queen, working mother, spiritual leader, and a governor. She influences not only the king and the army, she leads the people spiritually. She and Ahab are the classic power couple. Dual incomes. Both spouses working outside the home. Potential to influence each other and lead together.

But one thing is dead wrong. Jezebel's heart. She is evil to the core. There are few women in recorded history who match her darkness. As much as we try, we can't find a modern counterpart:

> In her evil power over her husband, Jezebel might
> be compared to Shakespeare's Lady MacBeth.
> In her fanaticism, she might be likened to Mary,
> Queen of Scots. Her death, though far more bitter
> and bloody, suggests the death on the guillotine of

another alien queen, Marie Antoinette. And like
Catherine de' Medici, Jezebel is remembered as
an outstanding example of what a woman ought
not to be.[4]

In society today, we try to separate our work from our spiritual
existence. *Sure, he may be an immoral guy, but he's really a fair
boss. It's no one's business what she does with her personal life
so long as she doesn't bring it into the office. Faith and work are
really two separate parts of life, and we need to keep it that way.*
Yet Jezebel proves that our true character tends to show up in
our actions—both at home and at work. It's not really possible to
separate our spiritual life from our daily work. Nor it is advisable.
Our hearts determine our actions.

Some Modern-Day Excuses for Evil

Did Jezebel really have a fair chance? She doesn't exactly grow up
in a loving home. She doesn't have a strong female role model.
Women in her time don't typically rule, and she has to learn a
few things on the job. She is under a lot of pressure. She has big
shoes to fill. Daddy never approved of her, and she has to show
him that she too can rule. No one teaches her about the God of
the Bible. She grows up thinking temple prostitution is normal.
Maybe she is even prostituted and exploited as a child. She is
likely tortured by the demons of her past, and she doesn't know
how to lead a nation, let alone how to recognize the voice of God.

Excuses, excuses. I can think of lots of reasons why Jezebel's
work went wrong. I even start to feel a bit sorry for her when I
imagine her life. There's no way she could have been happy. Yet

I'm reminded by the examples of other women—other working women of the Bible—that God gives us all grace. How we respond is up to us.

Eve, Rahab, and Ruth have already taught us about second chances. Before we finish Jezebel, I'd like to take a quick detour and focus on another woman. A woman whose story appears in the midst of Jezebel's reign.

SAME TIME, DIFFERENT RESPONSE

The widow of Sidon also appears in the book of the Kings.[5] She doesn't even have a name. She's just a widow living in Sidon, Jezebel's hometown. She doesn't have a title or a position. She doesn't have hope or confidence in the future, let alone confidence in herself. She doesn't have food, and she doesn't even have a husband. She's a single mom getting ready to make her last meal for her son and die of starvation.

The deck is stacked against her.

Like Jezebel, she is confronted by the prophet Elijah. And he asks her to do something really outrageous. He asks her to feed *him* with her last bit of flour. Mind you, this woman has no reason to believe in the God of Israel. Like Jezebel, she has grown up in a culture that worships Baal, exploits women, and endorses temple prostitution. For a woman of low standing, she may even be forced to prostitute to survive. She likely doesn't have positive role models or a godly upbringing. Maybe she is a victim of sexual exploitation or abuse. Yet for reasons I can't explain, the widow of Sidon chooses to follow Elijah's instruction. She has no reason to hope, yet she places her faith in the God of Israel.

Author Virginia Stem Owens provides remarkable insight into this unnamed woman:

> Why is this nameless woman introduced in the middle of Jezebel's story? Because the widow's extreme poverty and remarkable graciousness toward Elijah serve as a foil to the queen's opulence and arrogance. Though the woman comes from the same Sidonian culture as Jezebel, she is able to transcend that background and grasp the Living God. She is not culturally bound. Even the women who worship Jezebel's goddess can escape their own degradation and the destruction of their children when their hearts are open.[6]

I find the widow of Sidon compelling for several reasons. First and foremost, she is both humble and open. She doesn't have it all figured out. And just when she is about to give up, she opens herself to a miracle by simple obedience. As she prepares her last bit of food for Elijah, her resources multiply. Her flour and oil do not run dry, and she has enough food to provide for Elijah, herself, and her son to withstand the famine.

JEZEBEL'S CHOICE

So too, Jezebel has a choice.

I personally think her crossroads occurs at Mount Carmel. Let's face it, when fire comes down from heaven and your workforce of prophets is exterminated, isn't it time to make a change? For most of us, this would be a serious wake-up call. But not for Jezebel. She doesn't even contemplate a new plan. She is too proud and too entrenched. She can't see past herself, and she refuses to risk her power and position. Her heart actually gets harder.

It's hard to understand her resolve. Maybe she is in so deep that she can't fathom redemption. She is on the ultimate power trip, and Elijah is nothing more than a threat to her authority. While we'll never understand the complexity of the human heart, history shows us that position and power can be the very things that keeps us from giving God full reign, especially when it comes to our work.

Jezebel shows that absolute power corrupts absolutely. Putting her faith in God means giving up control. And sometimes, when we're in complete control—when we're used to getting our way—there is no turning back. Especially when you're the queen, the governor, and the CEO.

LETTING GO OF OUR KINGDOMS

Some of us can relate to Jezebel more than we care to admit. We cling to our security and tell God not to interfere with, let alone transform, our work. We contemplate giving God control of our homes and churches, but we don't even entertain the thought of letting him into our work. It is the final frontier of surrender. We enjoy earthly position and resources. People tend to respect us, and we'd like to keep it that way. Don't get me wrong, we don't have kingdoms and subjects and temple prostitutes to manage. But we each have our own "kingdom," and we don't want to let go.

Others of us have more in common with the widow of Sidon. We don't have resources. But we have plans to protect what we have. To make our last meal and eat every crumb ourselves—or maybe share it with our own families. But that's it. We don't plan on dividing the pie any further. Why be gracious in our work when there isn't enough to go around?

The widow of Sidon defies our self-protective nature. She has a small domain, yet she is willing to share. She shows us it's not about our position, our resources, or our culture. It's about our hearts. The irony here is that, in letting go, she gains a miracle. She bakes her last cake for Elijah, thinking she will never eat again. But God continues to fill the flour and oil, and she feeds her son through the famine.

Like these two very different women—Jezebel and the widow of Sidon—we all come to a crossroads. And we all have our own excuses. Regardless of our past, we have a choice. A chance to set our courses for the future. To make our work something that will honor God. To open our hearts and let go of our kingdoms. Will we trust God to direct our work, or will we take matters into our own hands?

The tragedy of Jezebel boils down to this. She isn't willing to let go of her kingdom. Are you?

Discussion Questions for Chapter Five

1. Can you think of a modern-day counterpart to Jezebel? Do you think she ever contemplated using her position for good?

2. Compare Jezebel's plight with the widow of Sidon. What are their differences? What are their similarities?

3. Have you reached a crossroads in your life where you feel that God is urging you to change direction? What can you learn from the widow of Sidon? From Jezebel?

4. Is God asking you to let go of your kingdom?

ನಿ *Select readings:* 1 Kings 16:29–19:18

CHAPTER FIVE NOTES

1. 1 Kings 16:29–19:18; 2 Kings 9.

2. The chapter on Jezebel in Virginia Stem Owens, *Daughters of Eve: Seeing Ourselves in Women of the Bible* (Colorado Spring, CO: NavPress, 2007) is a well-written and thorough read of Jezebel's story. I'll refer to it throughout this chapter, but it's definitely worth an independent read.

3. Owens, *Daughters of Eve*, 181.

4. Edith Deen, *All the Women of the Bible* (New York: Harper One, 1988), 126.

5. 1 Kings chapter 17.

6. Owens, *Daughters of Eve*, 183.

Chapter Six

HULDAH
Building a Solid Reputation

Most of us will never be famous. We think that God won't
use our work, simply because we're not well known. Our
jobs are too small. No one has ever asked us to do anything
important. Why should we expect any different?

Yet often God uses the quiet and faithful for greatness. I'd
like to introduce you to Huldah. She inspires the unknown.

You've probably never heard of her. I've yet to see Huldah
featured in a women's Bible study or a Sunday school curriculum.
Probably because she's inconspicuous and unassuming. And she
follows a few powerhouses in the book of the Kings like Deborah
and Jezebel. So she's easy to overlook.

Huldah isn't famous.

Yet her story is short and powerful. She's both a wife and
prophet. She's called upon during a time when the people desperately need to hear from God. And she's called upon because
of one reason: her reputation.

A woman's reputation is tough to build. And easy to lose.

WEATHERING THE REPUTATIONAL WARS

The events of the 2008 presidential campaigns show us the media is harder—we are harder—on female candidates. We want to talk about their mistakes, their outfits, their Botox (or lack thereof). We don't spend enough time valuing their reputations or listening to what they have to say.

I vividly recall sitting with a group of male lawyers who were ranting and raving about Hillary Clinton and Sarah Palin. But it wasn't the political discussion that bothered me. In fact, I don't even know which political party these guys supported or what they thought about the issues. They were too busy lamenting over why Clinton never wears skirts and taking shots at Palin for attending a community college rather than a "real" institution.

I had to leave the room. I'm not here to judge, just to make an observation. Famous or not, professional women are unfairly scrutinized by men and women alike. For most women, building—and maintaining—a solid reputation is an uphill battle.

And it's not just famous women who face this scrutiny. I think back to the girls in high school who lost the reputational wars at an early age, often unfairly. Decades later, these same women are connecting with former classmates on Facebook. What's the first thing that comes to mind when we see that "friend" request pop up? We don't care if she's a successful wife, mother, and upstanding member of the community. We can't forget her blunder at the junior prom!

Unfortunately, old reputations die hard.

We don't talk about this issue enough, especially in our faith communities. Which is why I want to pay more attention to women who have weathered the reputational wars.

Huldah is at the top of my list.

THE BOY KING SETS THE STAGE

In order to understand just how remarkable her reputation is, it helps to understand the world as Huldah knows it. Huldah lives during a period of turmoil and paganism. There is no stability, no moral authority, and certainly no respect for God. Yet in the midst of the chaos, God raises up an unlikely candidate for king: an eight-year-old boy, Josiah.

King Josiah is key to Huldah's story. He takes the throne sometime in the seventh century BC. And he sets out, even at an early age, to lead the people back to God.

Josiah's faith is worth some study. To start, he doesn't have the A-team of male role models. Let's look at the lineup. Josiah's father, King Amon, is as wicked as they come. He is remembered most for his idolatry and the revolt against him that leads to his assassination.

Josiah's grandfather, King Manasseh, set the stage for his son. He introduced pagan worship into the temple and abandoned the reforms of his own father.

Talk about a checkered past. Yet Josiah doesn't walk in the ways of his father or grandfather. We naturally question his foundation. Why does he want to follow God when the men around him embrace evil?

THE WOMAN BEHIND THE KING

Enter the Queen Mother.

Josiah learns to rely a great deal on his mother Jedidah, the queen. We don't know much about her—we do know that her husband, King Amon, is murdered in his own palace by his servants during a coup. So Queen Jedidah is likely terrified that her son will be the next casualty. Yet that doesn't stop her. She teaches Josiah to respect God and be the best he can be. She's the kind of mother who doesn't give up, even when circumstances are daunting and unpredictable. She could have thrown in the towel. She could have protected her son and discouraged him from leadership, especially after her husband is thrown from power. But she presses on and molds her son to lead a nation.

The result? Not only does Josiah seek to follow God, he also has a healthy respect for the role of women in God's kingdom. His upbringing and the influence of his mother help him value women in leadership. And so, when King Josiah is presented with a critical question of spiritual significance, he calls upon a prophetess to answer—Huldah.

Just before Huldah enters the scene (probably when he is a young man), Josiah commissions the people to rebuild and repair the temple. It is likely in complete disarray due to years and years of neglect. In the process of repairing the temple, the high priest Hilkiah discovers a lost scroll, probably the book of Deuteronomy. The high priest gives the scroll to Shaphan, the king's general or secretary of state. Shaphan reads the scroll aloud to the king.

"Great is the LORD's anger that burns against us because our fathers have not obeyed the words of this book; they have not acted in accordance with all that is written there concerning us."[1]

It's not good news. When Josiah hears it, he is shocked and shaken. The words cut like a knife. The law is clear. The people have disobeyed. And the Lord is angry.

WHY NOT PICK A MAN FOR THE JOB?

At this point, King Josiah tears his robes. He is more than distraught, but he also moves into action. Notice he doesn't ask the high priest to authenticate the scroll. Nor does the high priest offer. Perhaps he is ignorant. If so, what a shame. This shows us how bad things have gotten. Can't the high priest recognize moral authority when he sees it? Isn't that his full-time job? It's like the pastor of a church not being able to identify the Gospels as the eyewitness accounts of Jesus's life.

Or perhaps the high priest is simply unwilling. Maybe he knows exactly what has been found. He knows the words all too well, and he knows that Israel continues to violate every rule in the book. How can he deliver such terrible news to the King? No one wants to hear that his kingdom is full of moral depravity and destruction.

Whether the high priest is ignorant or unwilling, Josiah doesn't have full confidence in his services. He needs a second opinion. He wants a true expert, someone he trusts and respects, to validate and authenticate the most important discovery of his lifetime. After all, this is new material. If his current spiritual advisors knew about the law, they had conveniently failed to bring it to his attention. This perhaps raises a red flag and leads the king to seek counsel outside of his inner circle.

WHY PICK AN UNKNOWN WOMAN?

Without hesitation, Josiah sends the high priest, Hilkiah, to consult Huldah. They consult her at her home in the second quarter of Jerusalem. The second quarter is the section in front of the temple. This quarter has also been translated "in the college"—the Hebrew word is *mishneh*, meaning "place of repetition." Since education is often an oral affair in the ancient world, tradition is such that Huldah is some kind of teacher. "It is possible that Huldah's career involved some sort of official position in the temple, since the Mishnah—a compilation of Jewish commentary and traditions completed in about 200 CE—states that the two southern gates to the temple mount were called the Huldah Gates."[2]

We also know that Huldah is the wife of Shallum. His job is keeping the wardrobe—either for the priest or king. This would have placed his family close to the life of the temple and palace.

We don't know much more about Huldah's background. Like I said, she's not exactly famous. But King Josiah obviously has her on speed dial.

We already know that Josiah values spiritually discerning women, so he's not hung up on gender. He doesn't exclude Huldah simply because she is a woman. Note that other prophets are living at this time—including Habakkuk and Zephaniah. Both of these men have entire books of the Bible named after them. And we know that Zephaniah happens to be the king's close advisor.[3] Yet for reasons we're about to discover, Josiah chooses Huldah—not one of the guys—as the chosen expert.

Josiah doesn't choose Huldah because she is a woman. But he also doesn't exclude her because she is a woman. He picks her based on qualifications. He knows he needs to hear from God. He doesn't need a yes-man. And Huldah's reputation speaks for itself.

The king needs her expertise. He needs her experience. He needs her authority.

EXPERTISE TAKES TIME

Huldah works for years and years to establish her expertise. Probably unnoticed. She studies the law during a time when most of her countrymen don't even know it exists, let alone how to follow it. Besides, women have no formal education or positions of spiritual authority in her culture. Even if she learns the law, it's not like anyone will listen to her. Sure, she has heard (and likely taught) the stories about Deborah, but Deborah is the exception, not the norm. Huldah doesn't expect God to use her to do anything important.

In Huldah's world, there is no upward mobility for a woman who devotes her life to learning scripture. She's in a dead-end career. She'll likely teach children (and maybe a few women under the table) for the rest of her life. She'll hit the glass ceiling standing on her knees. So why does she bother?

I believe Huldah genuinely loves learning. She isn't satisfied with scratching the surface. She loves the Word of God. She wants to learn more. She embraces study based on sheer passion.

I'm not saying teaching children isn't important work. As far as I'm concerned, children are the best pupils and our most strategic investment. I have taught children's Sunday school for years, and it's the best Bible boot camp out there—for students and teachers.

But this is different. The king is requesting that Huldah—and no one else in his kingdom—identify a sacred book. This is serious business. This requires respect from the political *and* religious leaders. No room for error. No lightweights allowed.

Think about the training Huldah endured for this moment. It's one thing to read or study. It's another thing to become a true expert in a field. This type of expertise can take years to build. The king knows he needs someone with a scholar's familiarity of the ancient laws. The ancient laws are complicated and scholarship takes time.

Huldah doesn't become an expert overnight. There are no shortcuts. Head in the books. Nose to the grindstone. No one said it would be easy to master the ancient laws.

EXPERIENCE TAKES EVEN MORE TIME

The king doesn't just need expertise. Sometimes, knowledge isn't enough. We need to have applied knowledge to take it to the next level.

In other words, Huldah is more than book smart. She's not just an expert, she's a prophet. It's one thing to have knowledge. It's another thing to know what to do with it. And, yes, it's another thing to speak from God. Huldah may also be a teacher, and her experience with the wardrobes keeps her close to the life of the palace and the temple. She wasn't born yesterday.

She probably has a few gray hairs and maybe a few grown children. God places her in this position for a reason—perhaps this very moment.

We all know people who are "book smart" but who fail miserably in the real world. We also know people who get incredibly impatient working in support roles. People who think they know more and can do a better job than their bosses. Others are waiting for the big promotion or the "break" to be noticed.

Like it or not, experience involves waiting. When I first graduated from law school, prospective clients would all ask the same question. "How many years have you been practicing law?" They didn't want to know about my law school GPA or how well I did on the bar exam. They wanted to know about my experience working in the trenches. Of course, I found the question insulting, as do most new lawyers. But I learned to politely answer the question and wait for the gray hairs to emerge. And it taught me a valuable lesson. It takes time to develop a professional reputation.

Here's where Huldah is different from you and me.

Huldah doesn't just "put in her time" to gain respect and recognition. She develops her experience with no expectations. Her combined study and experience likely takes her years and years to develop. She likely knows she is smarter and more qualified than those in authority over her. Yet she continues to work hard with little hope for promotion.

She could have lost her patience. She might have even been past her prime. Certainly, she has been ready and waiting long enough.

Sometimes, when we're in the trenches, we tell God, "I'm ready. Now."

Huldah may have prayed this same prayer. But a promotion can be dependent on outside forces. To start, the king is finally ready. He now has the authority to rule and lead. Huldah may have been ready ten years ago, but she didn't have a king to support her. It's not like King Amon would have called Huldah a decade earlier.

Now is the time. Her experience will finally pay off. And Huldah is more than ready.

Authority Involves Answering the Question

The king needs someone who will speak truth and be accepted by the people. Someone who won't be afraid of what people think—someone who will get the people's attention. Someone who won't mince words.

No one else steps up to speak the truth into a bad situation. Not the high priest. Not the king's secretary. Not anyone in the king's inner circle. But Huldah is not afraid. She gets right to the point and exercises authority. First, she answers the question asked. She verifies the authenticity of the book—it is the Word of the Lord.

"This is what the Lord, the God of Israel, says: Tell the man who sent you to me, 'This is what the Lord says.'"[4]

Notice she first deals with the king's question. Clearly and directly. She doesn't go off on a tangent. She doesn't give a lengthy introduction or a political answer. She does the work she is specifically called to do.

Too often, we're so eager to do the work *we* want to do that we forget about the work in front of us. The work we are asked to do. It's only after we do our given job that we earn the respect to move up.

Huldah doesn't stop there. Yes, she does what she is asked to do, but she's not limited by her job description. She goes on to prophesy—something she wasn't asked to do. I love this balance between getting her work done and going beyond her work. Some of us only do what's inside the four corners of a job description—nothing more. Maybe we're afraid or lack confidence to step out. Others of us get ahead of ourselves. In doing more "important" work, we skip the job description all together. Yet Huldah shows we can accomplish both—we just need to do the work before us first.

DELIVERING A TOUGH MESSAGE

Huldah explains that God is angry at the people for worshipping other gods:

> "This what the LORD, the God of Israel, says:
> Tell the man who sent you to me, 'This is what
> the LORD says: I am going to bring disaster on
> this place and its people, according to every-
> thing written in the book the king of Judah has
> read. Because they have forsaken me and burned
> incense to other gods and provoked me to anger
> by all the idols their hands have made, my anger
> will burn against this place and will not be
> quenched.'"[5]

Then, Huldah speaks directly to the king,

"Tell the king of Judah, who sent you to inquire
of the LORD, 'This is what the LORD, the God
of Israel, says concerning the words you heard:
Because your heart was responsive and you hum-
bled yourself before the LORD when you heard
what I have spoken against this place and its
people, that they would become accursed and
laid waste, and because you tore your robes and
wept in my presence, I have heard you, declares
the LORD. Therefore I will gather you to your
fathers, and you will be buried in peace. Your
eyes will not see all the disaster I am going to
bring on this place.'"[6]

The text is silent hereafter regarding Huldah. She doesn't show
up again in the Bible. No mention, no shout-out, no "What
would Huldah think?" Yet we know that God uses her words.
She speaks a message that changes the spiritual and moral con-
sciousness of the people and sets the course for a king.

What's the key to delivering a tough message? Huldah makes
it clear she doesn't come in her own authority. The words are
God's words, and she is simply a messenger. Here, being a prophetess of God means speaking directly and boldly to the king.
Sometimes, the truth hurts. But speaking the truth is the very
thing that sets her apart.

BUT NOBODY KNOWS ME!

Huldah's quiet strength is easy to overlook. She doesn't have
the valor of Deborah. She doesn't have the drama of Rahab. She

doesn't have the authority of Jezebel. And she may not show up as the lead character in Sunday school lessons for years to come.

Yet we admire her all the more. Most of us, like Huldah, will never be famous. Her path to building a solid reputation is one that we can readily model.

We first must know what we're talking about. Pursue excellence. Gain expertise. Even if it takes time (too much time!). Then we must slog through the mud and put one foot in front of the other. It's called experience. There's no quick-fix solution or crash course to building an impeccable reputation. It's not like Huldah becomes a renowned scholar overnight.

And, like Huldah, there will be a time for action. A time for going outside our job descriptions. Maybe even a time for prophecy. Famous or not, we've got to be ready. Our reputations are worth building.

Wouldn't you like your opinion to be sought by a king?

Discussion Questions for Chapter Six

1. Do you agree that most of us are harder on women? Who are some modern-day women with desirable reputations?

2. Have you or someone close to you weathered a reputational challenge? What did you learn in the process?

3. How have you built expertise or experience in your work? Have you ever felt frustrated or impatient—that no one notices your value?

4. Do you ever struggle with knowing when and how to go outside of your job description? What can you learn from Huldah?

ঞ *Select readings:* 2 Kings chapter 22

CHAPTER SIX NOTES

1. 2 Kings 22:13.
2. Rose Sallberg Kam, *Their Stories, Our Stories: Women of the Bible* (New York: Continuum, 1995), 144 (citing Middoth 1.3, cited in Miriam Therese Winter, *WomanWisdom*, [New York: Crossroad Publishing Company, 1991], 336).
3 Owens, *Daughters of Eve*, 227.
4. 2 Kings 22: 15–16.
5. 2 Kings 22: 15–17.
6. 2 Kings 22:18–20.

THE WIDOW IN DEBT

Giving What We Have

n the book of Kings we read about a single mother who is about to lose everything. She can't pay her bills after her husband, a prophet, dies unexpectedly. And the creditors aren't just going to take her house, they are going to take what she loves most, her sons, if she can't pay up.

Listen to her agony as she pleads with Elisha the prophet: "'Your servant my husband is dead, and you know that he revered the LORD. But now his creditor is coming to take my two boys as his slaves.'"[1]

Things don't get much worse. She doesn't just have a problem. She has a crisis. I can't imagine the pit in her stomach or the feeling of helplessness.

What's a widow with no income, no leverage, and no resources supposed to do next? It's bad enough to lose your husband. It's another thing to lose your children in the process.

The word *widow* in Hebrew, pronounced *al-maw-naw*, literally means "an empty house." In other words, she is alone—both physically and emotionally. Her sons are her only family (not to mention her only form of support), and if they are ripped from her home she will lose everything.

Should we blame her late husband for her plight? From the text, we can assume he was a decent man. He "revered the LORD" even if his bank account wasn't very impressive. I don't think prophets earned much income in those days. Chances are, if he was hanging around Elisha, he was probably running from the authorities. Maybe he was an absent father or a careless spender. We'll never know. What we do know is that sometimes bad things happen to people who follow God, and life doesn't work out as planned. And regardless of how she got here, this widow is stuck. Her house is empty.

Yet she isn't ready to give in. She isn't ready to die with an empty house, and she certainly isn't ready to lose hope. What she lacks in resources, she makes up in fierce determination. In six short verses we're going to see how God transforms her work and turns a crisis into a miracle.

ANOTHER WILD PROPHET IN THE BOOK OF KINGS?

Some of you are ready to move on. You're getting tired of the book of Kings. I get it. But we can't afford to miss this one. The widow in debt has more in common with many of us than we may know, even if she lives in the ninth century BC.

Before we turn to the widow, it helps to understand another important character on the scene: the prophet Elisha.

Elisha is not to be confused with Elijah. It's a common mistake. They're both prophets. They both perform miracles and help widows. They both challenge authority and make lots of trouble.

In other words, Elijah and Elisha are cut from the same mold. This shouldn't surprise us since Elijah is Elisha's mentor. In fact, Elisha watches God take Elijah up to heaven, and it is said he received a "double portion" of Elijah's spirit.[2] Elisha is what we call double trouble.

Like Elijah, Elisha is committed to truth and justice. He speaks his mind. He tends to make a scene and has no tact. If we read the prior chapters of Kings, we know that Elisha is likely an accomplice to one of Elijah's last acts on this earth—repeatedly sending fire from heaven to torch the messengers of the king of Samaria, then prophesying and witnessing the king's death. Just a bit defiant, don't you think? After Elijah is taken up to heaven, Elisha doesn't miss a beat. He curses a group of youths for calling him a "baldhead," resulting in two bears emerging from the woods to defend Elisha (that was the end of the youths).[3] Next, when the king of Israel asks Elisha for help, he responds only after giving the king a piece of his mind: "if I did not have respect of Jehoshaphat king of Judah, I would not look at you or even notice you."[4]

If you're trying to win friends in high places, you don't go around insulting kings. But Elisha isn't worried about political and social influence. In fact, he has more enemies than friends—*especially* in high places. His sharp tongue and abrasive style (not to mention his "bald" head) make him downright offensive to the political and social elite.

Why is Elisha so important to the widow's story? We need to understand exactly to whom she is turning for help. For some reason, the widow seeks *him*. She doesn't hire a lawyer, shack up with a new man, or try to handle the matter on her own. She reaches out to a prophet. A crazy and hated prophet.

DESPERATE OR FAITHFUL?

What could she possibly be thinking? She's either incredibly faithful or incredibly desperate. Or both. Sometimes the two go hand in hand.

I happen to think she knows about the "double portion." Remember when Elisha watches a chariot take Elijah to heaven? The "company of prophets" is also waiting in the distance. Could it be that her late husband is among this audience—and that he later tells his wife of the fiery chariot and the power of God?

This woman knows she needs more than friends in high places. She needs the One in high places. So she boldly contacts Elisha and tells him like it is. She doesn't mince words. She even implies that he bears some responsibility for her plight.

"'*Your* servant my husband is dead, and you know that he revered the LORD.'"[5]

In other words, *My husband spent all that time running around with the company of prophets, and look where it got him! You're the one who got him into this mess!*

THE HEALING POWER OF WORK

Elisha listens. He doesn't blame her for being angry. He's empathetic, but he also squarely puts the responsibility for her family back in her hands. He asks her what she has to give.

"How can I help you? Tell me, what do you have in your house?"[6]

My first reaction is one of surprise. We know that widow means "empty house." Elisha certainly knows her house is empty—that she has nothing to give. So why does he bother to ask? Is he trying to insult her?

Elisha isn't a sensitive guy to begin with. He obviously skipped Grief Counseling 101. And in our modern-day world he would be accused of being harsh and even calloused to her loss. Yet I firmly believe Elisha maintains this widow's dignity. He knows that healing comes not from what we receive but from what we give.

I'm not a specialist in grief. Just the opposite—I'm probably less experienced than Elisha. In fact, I used to walk on eggshells and pretend things were "normal" to cope with grief. And I used to think people grieving needed pity and empathy. Then I watched someone close to me suffer an unexpected and tragic loss. The last thing she wanted was people to feel sorry for her. She wanted to help herself and care for her family. She didn't want to be passive. Instead, she wanted and needed to take action—to get to work!

This is where Elisha is instrumental. He may look cold and insensitive on the outside, but inside he is wise and kind. Besides, he's never walked on eggshells, and he's never acted "normal." Why should he start now? He knows this widow doesn't need a pity party—she needs a plan. She wants and needs to take action. She doesn't want to be passive or dependent on others to fix her plight. But she is paralyzed by circumstances and needs a nudge.

So he does the unthinkable. Brilliant yet unthinkable. He calls her to work!

Elisha doesn't pity the widow or blame her late husband. He too wants her to be part of the solution. He knows the healing power of work—helping yourself, so that God can work in and through you. In calling the widow to work, he charges her to take action, to find the answers, to use her resources. He gives her permission to heal.

He also starts with what she has. He doesn't focus on what she doesn't have. He doesn't say, *Well, I can see that there is literally nothing in your house. But let's try to be positive here. Can't you pull yourself together?*

Instead he both offers to *help* and asks her what she has to *give.* He doesn't presume to know her needs. Yet he does expect her to work toward the solution.

Her initial response is classic. It's also the way most of us respond when God asks us what we have to give. Can you hear the indignant tone in her voice as she responds to what appears to be a stupid question: "Your servant has nothing there at all."[7]

I'VE GOT NOTHING TO GIVE GOD!

Can you relate to this widow? I can. Too many days, I feel like I have nothing to give. I admit, I feel silly complaining. I'm not a single parent or a widow. No one is threatening to take away my children, and I'm not living under the pressure of enormous debt or about to lose my house. But many days, I feel like my house is empty.

I struggle with the usual demands of home and work. Raising three school-aged children. Trying to maintain a healthy marriage. Running between after-school activities, homework, and carpool duty. Mediating sibling rivalry and slaying media dragons. Juggling a busy law practice that could take every hour of my day and trying to stay connected with friends, family, and a community of faith. Like this widow, I look in my cupboard after a long day and see nothing.

There is nothing left. I have nothing to give, God.

Yet this widow does something amazing. She goes back to her cupboard and looks again. She doesn't stop at nothing.

"Your servant has nothing there at all," she said, *"except a little oil."* [8]

Like so many of us, she is conflicted when she responds to God. She starts with an initial response of nothing, yet she acknowledges in the next breath she has something. In a matter of seconds, she changes course—she gets ready to work. She knows she has something to give.

Granted, it's a small jar. She almost overlooks it. It's not much. But she still offers it up. It's a resource. So she puts it on the table, not knowing what's next.

Okay, Maybe I Have a Little Oil

This is the defining moment. A breakthrough. It's the pivotal point that decides if she's open to a miracle. She likely doesn't know the importance of a little oil. But it's not the oil itself that is remarkable. It's her brave spirit—her commitment to work and contribute to the solution. So she puts her one and only resource on the table. And she doesn't just put it on the table for her family, she offers it to a wild prophet!

Elisha knows just what to do. He doesn't give her a handout. He gives her a plan and expects her to execute it. He quickly tells her to get to work. With God's help, he asks her to take responsibility for herself, her family, and even the debts of her late husband.

Elisha says, "'Go around and ask all your neighbors for empty jars. Don't ask for just a few. Then go inside and shut the door behind you and your sons. Pour oil into all the jars, and as each is filled, put it to one side.'"[9]

It's an unusual plan. He doesn't ask the debtors to cancel the debt. He doesn't try to get the town to pass the "widow bailout plan." He doesn't snap his fingers and make the oil appear.

In her mind, she is probably thinking, *this is completely ridiculous. Isn't there another way?* It's one thing to call her to action, but collecting jugs from the neighbors? This doesn't make any sense. Frankly, it would make more sense to ask the neighbors for a monetary contribution. Or ask them to put some oil in the pot. Or ask them to petition the town leaders for mercy and discharge her debt.

But collecting empty jugs?

She could have refused. She could have begged him for another plan—a plan that would involve somebody else paying her debt. A plan that would allow her to keep her oil—the only thing she has of any value. A plan that embraces more sensible work.

He's already asked her for what she has. Now he's asking her to go get something she doesn't have. And he's asking her to involve other people in this irrational scheme. Isn't this a bit much?

WORK FIRST, ASK QUESTIONS LATER

Yet she quickly gets to work. With her sons. She can save her questions for later.

The mother and her sons gather the jars, and they shut the door behind them. Without Elisha. After all, he clearly tells her to "shut the door." I think he wants them to tackle this crisis together—as a family. And he wants them to know that God is the source of this miracle—not him—so he intentionally stays behind. So the widow follows Elisha's direction.

Then she starts to pour the oil. It keeps flowing. Jar after jar is full. She says to her son, "'Bring me another one.'"

But he replies, "'There is not a jar left.'" Then the oil stops flowing.[10]

I love how she involves her sons in this work. They have already experienced loss, and getting their hopes up is risky. Maybe they are already questioning Elisha. What if his plan doesn't work? There are no other options in sight. Both she and her sons will be devastated. It's like telling your kids to put out their stockings on Christmas Eve, not knowing whether there will be presents in the morning. No mother wants to set up her children for disappointment. Especially when they have already been hurt. But she doesn't let this fear stop her.

Notice how the oil doesn't stop until the jars are gone. God keeps the oil flowing until the last jar is full. He doesn't pull the plug prematurely. The more jars she brings to the table, the more he will fill. He only stops when she stops. And while we may limit God in our work, this miracle shows us that he doesn't limit us. He doesn't say, *No more! I can't make any more oil!* Instead, he multiples the oil—enough to pay her debts and then some.

CAN MY ORDINARY WORK BECOME A MIRACLE?

The widow is like the boy with five loaves and two fish. Could Jesus have fed five thousand people another way? Absolutely. Yet he focuses on what the boy has to give—five loaves and two fish. Like the widow, the boy gives what he has, and God uses it for something greater. Jesus multiplies the fish and bread—and the baskets of food keep flowing. The flow doesn't stop until every stomach is full.

Could Jesus have bypassed the disciples and multiplied the bread and fish with a snap of his fingers? Absolutely. Yet he chose to use the hands and feet of the disciples. He tells them, "You give them something to eat" and in doing so their work is part of a miracle.[11]

God likewise uses the hands and feet of the widow and her sons. Just picture them going door to door, collecting empty jugs and not knowing the result. Imagine their surprise when what seemed like an ordinary task—pouring oil into empty jugs—becomes part of a miracle.

Most of us are completely closed to miracles. Especially in our daily work. We stop short of putting our oil on the table. We don't see the bread and fish in our lunch, and we feel like we have nothing to give. We would never entertain the thought of giving away our only resources—especially to a crazy and hated prophet. So we sit back and play it safe. And we wonder where God is and why he doesn't seem to care.

In the process, we miss the miracle. Don't get me wrong, God can act with or without our oil. But I worry that we don't even know what we're missing. Yet if we're really honest, deep in our hearts we long for a miracle. We desperately *need* a miracle. We wonder, *is it really possible?*

The widow and the small boy show us where to start.

Ask. Give. Believe.

Can it really be this simple?

THE COURAGE TO ASK

It must have been terribly hard for the widow to ask Elisha for help. The first step is often the most difficult. Yet asking the question is crucial to the story. If she doesn't ask, there's no miracle. Asking involves humility. Putting aside her pride and admitting she can't handle the crisis alone.

Asking is a process. There are two pieces that must come together. Once we find the courage to ask, the second step is just as important—we have to know *who* to ask. It's one thing knowing you need help. But if you seek out wrong advice, you can end up worse off. Getting the right (or wrong) advice can change everything. In the widow's case, if she seeks out wrong advice, she will miss a miracle.

In asking a prophet to help, she shows us that sometimes we don't need a business or political advisor to sort out a mess. We need a spiritual solution. This cuts against our tendency to seek out an expert with power, respect, or authority. Someone with social connections or political solutions. A prophet is none of these things. A prophet isn't going to tell us what we want to hear. More often than not, he's going to tell us what we don't want to hear. His only qualification is his direct access to God— his ability to speak from God to the people.

I'm not saying to avoid experienced advisors in our work. But it's easy to avoid the "prophets" around us simply because we don't want to hear what they have to say—we'd rather have a worldly solution. Why risk that God will ask us to do something crazy? Like go around and fill up empty jars for a living. Yet God often places an "Elisha" in our lives for a reason. Like the widow, we need to hear from God. And we need to ask.

GIVING WHAT WE HAVE

Once we ask, God will likely turn the tables. What do we have to give? He'll probably tell us to get to work and to use our resources as part of the solution. Yet God typically isn't asking us to risk everything. He's asking us—like the widow—to start with what we have.

It's easy to focus on what we don't have. *I don't have financial security. I don't have a husband to support me. I don't have an advanced degree. I don't have respect in the community. I don't have resources or position. My house is empty.*

Yet when we focus on what we have to give, everything changes. It's not up to us anymore, it's up to God. Like the widow, we put our oil on the table. Like the little boy, we reach into our pockets and give Jesus our lunch. No, it's not much. But it doesn't have to be. In giving God what we have, we don't refuse the work God puts before us. It doesn't matter if the work is beneath us. It doesn't matter if it's not what we had in mind. Pouring oil into empty jugs doesn't make any sense. But God is in the business of starting small and going big—which sometimes means starting by opening up the cupboard.

CONFLICTED BELIEF

Some of us wouldn't recognize a miracle if it hit us upside the head. We're hanging on so tightly to our resources that there's just no room for God. We're playing it too safe.

Or we simply lack faith. We want to believe, but our circumstances seem impossible. And, like the widow, we're conflicted. In the same breath, we tell God we have nothing and something. How can we possibly overcome our unbelief when we can't even make up our minds?

The widow shows us it's okay to be conflicted. She doesn't have it figured out when she asks for help. God isn't surprised at her confusion, and he uses her fickle heart. He even rewards her reluctant faith.

God isn't surprised by our confusion either. He calls us to action, even as we struggle to believe. Isn't action the pivotal moment of faith? Like the widow, we believe by putting our oil on the table. We still have doubts, but we're not paralyzed by unbelief. We tell God that we live in a conflicted state, and we ask Him to help. Like the young father asking Jesus to heal his son, we tell God, "I do believe; help me overcome my unbelief!" [12]

I used to think it was all or nothing. Doubt or faith; how can the two possibly coexist? Yet like the young father, I find myself praying a conflicted prayer. My motives are mixed and my faith is weak. *I believe God, but it's really hard. So please help me overcome my unbelief.*

WHAT DO YOU HAVE IN YOUR HOUSE?

In the midst of my struggles, I too ask for help. And, like the widow, I can hear God responding,

How can I help you? Tell me, what do you have in your house?

My initial response?

Nothing. I have absolutely nothing, God. Every inch of me is committed to a carpool schedule, a billable hour, a lunch that needs packing, a shirt that needs folding. I have given everything I have to give!

Yet the widow doesn't stop at nothing. How can I? So I go back to the cupboard and look. I realize that I too have a little oil in my house. In fact, I have more than a little oil. In addition to the basic necessities of food, family, and shelter, I have more luxuries than this widow or the rest of the world will ever know.

I can't stop at nothing. I have so much more to give.

Discussion Questions for Chapter Seven

1. When you're in a crisis, to whom do you turn for help? Why do you think the widow asks Elisha?

2. Notice how Elisha deals with the widow's grief. What can we learn from his approach? Have you ever experienced the healing power of work?

3. Do you find yourself living in a conflicted state of doubt and belief? How can we resolve this tension?

4. Do you feel your house is empty? Take another look in your cupboard. What are all the resources you have to bring to the table?

8 *Select readings:* 2 Kings chapter 4

CHAPTER SEVEN NOTES

1. 2 Kings 4:1.
2. 2 Kings 2:9.
3. 2 Kings 2: 23–25.
4. 2 Kings 3:14.
5. 2 Kings 4:1 (emphasis added).
6. 2 Kings 4:2.
7. Ibid.
8. Ibid. (emphasis added).
9. 2 Kings 4:3–4.
10. 2 Kings 4:6.
11. Luke 9:13.
12. Mark 9:24.

ESTHER
Embracing Our Destiny

'm sitting on a large piece of shag carpet watching my Sunday school teacher put up a picture of a beautiful queen on a felt board. She's dressed in purple. She wears a crown with matching gold wristbands, and she has long, flowing black hair. She looks a lot like Wonder Woman, and I'm pleased to finally see a female superhero in the Bible. Most of my Sunday school lessons are about men. But not this one. So I pay attention closely. The story goes something like this:

"A nice Jewish girl wins a beauty contest and becomes queen of Persia. She goes to live in the palace with the king and soon discovers an evil and secret plot to destroy the Jews. She is very brave. She persuades the king to protect the Jews and saves her people. She rides into the sunset and lives happily ever after. Every little girl should aspire to be like Esther."

Esther doesn't disappoint. She soon becomes my favorite Bible heroine, and I beg my mother to read me her story over and over again. I am mesmerized by her beauty. I marvel at her bravery. My favorite part is when she risks her life to approach the king—even though the law states that the penalty for approaching him in the royal throne room without an invitation is death. Yet Esther isn't afraid. Of course the king listens to her and makes an exception to the silly law. Esther saves the day and rescues her people. She isn't just beautiful. She's smart, gutsy, and persuasive. I want to grow up and be just like Esther.

Now that I'm older, I can see that Esther's story is no fairy tale. It's more like a nightmare. And, when I read the rest of the story (including the messy parts), I marvel all the more at this brave woman. She has her work cut out for her. Or maybe she is cut out for her work.

A Woman in Hiding

Before Esther becomes a queen, she is hidden. Esther doesn't set out for public service. It's not like she has royal blood, and she certainly isn't in training for palace life. To the contrary, becoming queen of Persia is probably the farthest thing from her mind. As a Jew living in exile, Esther is just trying to survive.

Esther is an orphan. And her real name isn't Esther. She conceals her given name, Hadassah, likely to hide her Jewish identity. She is raised by her cousin Mordecai and is likely the second or third generation of her family living in exile. It's during a time when Persians dominated the entire Middle East, and Esther is living in the city of Susa, somewhere in southwestern Iran. Her parents or grandparents were likely exiled from Jerusalem in 586 BC after the Babylonian conquest. Cyrus the Great of Persia permits Jews to return to their homeland in 539 BC. Yet several decades later, Esther and Mordecai remain in

ESTHER: Embracing Our Destiny

Persia.[1] Maybe life in Persia wasn't so bad after all—and since Esther is hidden, she likely blends right in. She talks, dresses, and looks like a Persian.

Esther has several meanings—all of which are potentially significant. One derivation of Esther is *Ishtar*, the goddess of love. Is Esther hiding behind the name of a pagan god? Or does she bear the name Esther because of its close relation to the Hebrew word for "hidden," *Satar*? This is more consistent with her hidden identity. Yet another derivation of Esther is *Stara*, the Persian word for "star."[2] Esther is like a glow stick—you can't turn her off.

Regardless of the origin of her name, one thing is clear. Esther sets out to lead a hidden life and fly under the radar. She probably hopes to marry a nice Jewish boy and earn a modest living.

But a knock-out like Esther can't hide her light under a bushel. Some women just can't keep a low profile. She has a presence that commands attention. When she walks into a room, everyone notices. The great irony here is that this woman who is trying to hide her identity soon becomes the most famous woman in all of Persia.

The Persian king Xerxes[3] (486–465 BC) is about to find a new wife. His old wife, Queen Vashti, is banished from the kingdom for refusing to parade around in front of his drunken friends. Let's just say King Xerxes has a bit of a temper. He likes his wine. He likes his women. And he doesn't like it when anyone disobeys his orders.

Just the kind of guy every woman doesn't want to end up with. But Esther doesn't have much of a choice. He tends to get what he wants.

THE UNTHINKABLE JOB INTERVIEW

One of my worst job interviews happened during law school. I was interviewing with an out-of-town law firm, and the guy questioning me didn't seem to care about my resume. He was more interested in my wedding ring.

He kept asking me if my husband was going to move out of town with me. Whether I was planning to have kids. What kind of work my husband did.

I couldn't get out of the interview fast enough. It was only thirty minutes. But it was still really uncomfortable. When I came home and told my husband about the interview, we both shook our heads. Does anyone really think a job depends on gender?

Nothing about Esther's job interview is comfortable. Everything about it is sexist. Not only will Esther be judged on her beauty, she will be judged on her sensuality for an entire evening.

To start, Esther is "gathered" by the king's men in search of a beautiful virgin. It's not like she voluntarily enters a beauty pageant. Does she really have a choice but to step up and participate in the "pageant" and throw herself at the mercy of the king?

She immediately enters beauty boot camp. No, this isn't charm school. This "internship" is led by the head of the king's harem, Hegai. Hegai takes a special liking to Esther, and he seems to give her some extra pointers on pleasing the king. Let's not go there, but I happen to think this internship involved more than beauty treatments.

Speaking of beauty treatments, the Persians know how to do it right. They spend more than a day at the spa. Beautiful women are important to the king, and he spares no resources. Money and time are no obstacles. Esther is given some twelve months of beauty treatments before she meets the king—six months of oil and myrrh and six months of perfume and cosmetics.

That's a lot of Botox.

And let's not forget that Esther receives personal coaching from Hegai. By the time Esther has her interview with the king, she is more than ready. The rules for the interview are clear. She is to go to the palace to meet the king in the evening. She can take with her whatever she needs. She will return to another part of the harem in the morning.

In other words, the king will make his decision based on a one-night stand. If Esther is chosen, she will become queen. If she is not, she will be a reject in the harem forever. It's all or nothing. So she steps up and plays the game.

Esther Plays the Game to Win

Esther doesn't just play the game. She plays to win. Is she motivated by sport or survival? We don't really know. What we do know is that she uses everything in her power—her natural beauty, her charm, and everything she has learned in her internship—to make her impression on the king.

The competition is tough. There are hundreds of beautiful virgins in Persia. They all want to be queen, and only one can win. This is reality TV at its best. The virgin pageant would no doubt be in instant hit. Viewers could watch the before and after shots of the beauty treatments and vote on the winner. Esther would undoubtedly have a huge following of fans. She somehow sets herself apart from the rest. Maybe it's her close relationship with Hegai—he likely gives her the inside scoop about the king. After all, Esther takes nothing with her to the interview except what Hegai advises and completely follows Hegai's instructions. She learns how to work the system. Esther is no stranger to office politics. She knows what she has to do to get ahead, and with singular focus and sheer talent she wins the competition.

The king places a gold crown on her head, and she proudly emerges as the new queen of Persia. The crowd cheers and she takes a bow. All of those beauty treatments paid off.

Or did they? We can only imagine her private thoughts. Is this really what she wants? There are too many unanswered questions.

IT'S LONELY AT THE TOP

Will this job really make her happy? Does she ask God to guide her as queen? Does she promise herself she won't get caught up in the immorality of palace life? Does she ever plan to disclose her true heritage?

We can't judge Esther, and we can't know her heart. She is likely conflicted. Yet she doesn't walk away from the game. She doesn't refuse to play on moral or religious grounds. She puts on the crown and wears it well. She accepts her position with grace and honor. I'm not saying it's an easy transition. She likely sobs in her bed at night, realizing she will never lead a normal life. She will forever share her husband with a harem. She will never have a home or a family to call her own.

So while Esther may have gone into the kingdom with a bang, she likely feels alone and deserted. Like she doesn't belong in the palace. Her position as queen of Persia pulls her far away from the life and soul of the Jewish people living in exile. And while there are many benefits to her work and position, she can't help but feel torn.

She is famous, yet she is hidden. She lives in the palace for the next five years, yet no one knows who she really is. Not even the king knows her true identity. Esther knows what it's like to hide her faith at work. Maybe she even enjoys playing the game—thinking it will last forever. Her work opens new doors. The more options she has, the harder it is to say no. The more luxuries she has, the harder it is to give them up. The more experiences she has, the harder it is to identify with her former life.

But things tend to come to a head when we are living in two worlds. Esther's worlds are about to collide. A plot is brewing inside the palace to destroy the Jews.

BEING AT THE RIGHT PLACE AT THE RIGHT TIME

Esther's cousin Mordecai is watching from a distance. He is looking out for Esther even before he learns of the plot to overthrow the Jews.

And it's a nasty plot. The king's chief advisor and right-hand man, Haman, hates the Jews with a passion. Haman's rage originates with Esther's cousin Mordecai. Mordecai won't pay homage to Haman or bow down to him, violating the king's orders. Haman is outraged—not just at Mordecai but at all the Jews. It may be that Haman and Mordecai have a family history, and Haman clearly sees the Jews as a threat to his existence. So he devises a plan to destroy them.

He approaches the king over some wine. He tells the king about this outrage. With the king's approval and authority,

Haman issues a declaration that the Jews will be destroyed. He casts a lot, or *pur*, to determine the day of destruction, arriving on the thirteenth day of the twelfth month, almost a year forward. He seals the edict with the king's signet ring. It's a done deal. Every Jew in the land will be eliminated. Haman is one of the first recorded anti-Semites.

The decree is published throughout the land. The Jews are devastated. And while the decree goes out on the eve of Passover, the Jews aren't feasting. They are wailing. Mordecai is clothed in sackcloth and ashes, and he goes out to the city crying bitterly. Esther doesn't even know what is bothering him. Is she living under a rock? How can she not know that her people are about to be destroyed? The fact that Esther doesn't know what is happening shows that she is living on a different planet. Her people are out of sight and out of mind.

Esther must step up. She must find out what is bothering Mordecai. So she sends out her messengers to find him. Mordecai doesn't mince words. In the seminal verse of the book—the turning point—he tells her she must arise and fight.

> "'Do not think that because you are in the king's house you alone of all the Jews will escape. For if you remain silent at this time, relief and deliverance for the Jews will arise from another place, but you and your father's family will perish. And who knows but that you have come to royal position for such a time as this?'"[4]

In a moment, her life is changed. She must make a choice and must do so quickly. Never mind how she got to be queen. Never mind that she slept her way to the top. Never mind that she made mistakes and concealed her true identity from everyone.

Esther is in this position for a reason. She is in the right place at the right time. She knows destiny when she sees it. She is the only person in the kingdom who can save her people. So she rises to the occasion.

Knowing How to Approach Your Boss

Approaching an unreasonable boss for a huge favor has its challenges. It's all about choosing the right words. Having the right tone. Waiting for the right moment.

Esther is asking for more than a raise, and we can learn much from her approach. Let's start with what she doesn't do. She doesn't rush. She doesn't run to the king when her emotions are high. She doesn't stomp her feet and whine.

Instead, she waits.

And she doesn't just wait. She fasts for three days. Her maids fast with her, and she instructs Mordecai and the Jews to do the same. If she's going to risk her life, she's not going to do it lightly. It is during this three-day period that Esther likely puts her plan together. She clears her head. She counts the cost.

Fasting and waiting give Esther time to think. She thinks about what she will do, but she also thinks about how the king will react. She knows he's a mean drunk. A moody and fickle man. How do you approach a volatile boss who doesn't have a great track record in dealing with women? She likely prays he will call her first, but he doesn't. Like many decisions in life, she must take the initiative. And, in this case, she must break the law to do so. She decides it is worth the risk. So she approaches the king in the royal throne room and risks death.

The king extends the golden scepter. She's in the door! Yet she still doesn't rush to plead her case. Instead, Esther teaches us how to have a critical conversation when the deck is stacked against us. To start, she speaks to the king in his own language: "'If it pleases the king, may the king and Haman come this day to the banquet that I have prepared for him.'"[5]

Her plan is brilliant. She knows the king likes to eat and drink. He's more likely to give her a favorable response when he is in a good mood. So she carefully sets the scene and positions her request.

As they drink at the banquet, the king asks Esther what she wants. He even offers her up to half the kingdom. But Esther still doesn't jump. She keeps the king in suspense.

> "My petition and my request is: if I have found
> favor in the sight of the king, and if it pleases the
> king to grant my petition and do what I request,
> may the king and Haman come to the banquet
> which I will prepare for them, and tomorrow I
> will do as the king says."[6]

The suspense is killing him. This is reverse psychology at its best. Notice she makes it all about him! She goes out of her way to be deferential. If she's going to get what she wants, the king is going to have to think it's his idea.

Talk about a woman with instincts. And patience. She knows the timing isn't quite right, so she waits *another* day.

Timing Is Everything

Over the evening, the king can't sleep. He is likely up worrying about Esther and her pending request. So he asks his advisors to bring him some bedtime reading material, and the book of records is read to the king.

God is about to show up. The king reads about an earlier event he had forgotten—Mordecai's work to uncover a plot to save the king's life. The king is troubled that Mordecai has never been honored, so he determines to make things right.

In one sleepless night, everything changes. Mordecai is elevated in the king's sight. Esther's clever work is about to pay off. The timing is finally right. The next evening, Esther sits at the palace in a *second* dinner with the king and Haman. This time, she boldly yet tactfully presents her case.

> "If I have found favor in your sight, O king, and
> if it pleases the king, let my life be given me as
> my petition, and my people as my request; for we
> have been sold, I and my people, to be destroyed,
> to be killed and to be annihilated. Now if we had
> only been sold as slaves, men and women, I would
> have remained silent, for the trouble would not be
> commensurate with the annoyance to the king."[7]

She continues to keep him in suspense. She carefully chooses her words. She is persuasive yet respectful. It is still all about him! She goes out of her way to let him know he need not be inconvenienced. She could have said, *Look, are you asleep at the switch? My people are going to die if you don't do something. You have to do something now!*

No, instead she keeps her cool and pushes the envelope gently but firmly. Her tact and strategy pay off. The king orders the death of Haman, honors Mordecai, and sides with the queen. Esther can breathe a sigh of relief and go back to her beauty treatments.

Or can she?

FINISHING THE JOB

When we read the rest of the story, we see that Esther's work is hardly done. It's not like the king sets everything right. Everything is still wrong. Sure, Haman is gone, but the edict still stands. An order with the king's signet ring can't be revoked. And the king has done nothing to help! Several months pass since Esther first approached the king, and she's right back where she started.[8]

Esther shows us that finishing a job is just as important as getting hired. It's one thing to be in a powerful position. It's another thing to get things done.

Esther risks her life a second time. She approaches the king in the royal throne room, and again he extends the golden scepter. This time, she is ready. Time is of the essence, so she gets right to the point. She asks for an order overruling Haman's edict.

This time, something remarkable happens. The king gives Esther full authority to write another decree. He even tells her to do it with his signet ring, "in the king's name in behalf of the Jews as seems best to you."[9] In other words, the king delegates to Esther and empowers her to act with his authority.

Esther doesn't waste a second. She uses her newfound power to empower the people. An edict is written permitting the Jews to protect themselves from the coming attack. She makes certain that the edict is written in the local language of each province "and also to the Jews in their own script and language."[10] She dots her i's and crosses her t's. Mordecai seals the edict with the signet ring and ensures it will be delivered promptly to every corner of the kingdom.

After the Jews successfully defend themselves, a celebration is in order. She now sets out to honor the people. The festival of Purim is established to remember this victory. Again, Esther is in full force. With the authority of her position, she makes the celebration official. She issues yet another decree and writes letters to all the Jews. She gives them words of "goodwill and assurance" and issues regulations to confirm the celebration of Purim for generations to come. In doing so, she not only finishes the job but she honors the people and makes it their victory—not hers. Her work is finally complete.

Or is it? We know from history that King Xerxes is later murdered in his bed. Esther likely has her hands full for years to come. Life in the palace is more than banquets and beauty treatments. Yet Esther now rules with her identity known to all. She isn't hiding anymore.

IMPERFECT BUT AVAILABLE

Esther shows us that imperfect, unexpected, and available women make history. This isn't the first time that God uses a woman who isn't religious or morally upright. In fact, he seems to delight in using such women to make history. As with Rahab and the widow in debt, Esther comes to a crisis—a place where she must choose her course. Forget the past. Forget her mistakes.

She is in this place for a reason. And God is more interested in the future.

Like these brave women, we've all gotten to this place in life for a reason. We've made a few mistakes along the way. We've made a few questionable career choices. We've made unhealthy alliances. We've taken advice from people like Hegai, and we've played office politics.

But we've also worked hard. We've dreamed big dreams. Life hasn't worked out exactly as planned, but we're not willing to throw away our positions. Nor should we.

Like Esther, we are imperfect. We are in need of grace. We live in two worlds and sometimes we forget our true identities. But our identities don't depend on who we are or what we do. Our identities depend on who God is and what he has done for us. He hasn't forgotten his children.

Like Esther, we too have a destiny. Will we be available? We may not have beauty, power, or position. But, like Esther, it's time to come out of hiding.

"And who knows but that you have come to royal position for such a time as this?"[11]

Discussion Questions for Chapter Eight

1. Can you relate to Esther's hidden identity? Have you ever hidden your faith at work?

2. Esther risks her life to approach the king. What can we learn from her preparation before she enters the throne room? What can we learn from her patience in preparing two banquets for the king and Haman?

3. Has God ever placed you in a position for a reason? Looking back, was it a position you sought or expected?

4. Esther uses her authority to empower and honor the people. What does this teach us about her leadership?

೫ *Select readings:* The book of Esther

CHAPTER EIGHT NOTES

1. James, *Lost Women of the Bible*, 144.

2. Donald E. Curtis, "Esther–Irony and Providnece," bible. org, accessed January 19, 2013, http://bible.org/seriespage/ esther-8211-irony-and-providence.

3. King Xerxes is referred to as King Ahasuerus in the book of Esther. The name Ahasuerus is equivalent to the Greek name Xerxes, and biblical scholars and historians generally recognize both as the same person.

4. Esther 4: 13–14.

5. Esther 5:4 (NASB).

6. Esther 5:7–8 (NASB).

7. Esther 7:3–4 (NASB).

8. Esther first approached the king in the month of Nisan. It is now the month of Sivan—three months later. See Curtis, "Esther–Irony and Providence," http://bible.org/seriespage/ esther-8211-irony-and-providence.

9. Esther 8:8.

10. Esther 8:9.

11. Esther 4:14.

PROVERBS 31
Can We Have It All?

s it really possible for women to have it all—thriving relationships, a healthy home, a booming career? If you ask women of faith this question, you'll get a host of possible answers. There's still a contingent inside the church that believes women are limited to traditional roles. *You can't be a devoted mother or wife and work outside your home. You can't work full time and give your family the attention they deserve. Day care will ruin your kids. Who do you want to raise your kids, a stranger or you?*

At the same time, there are a growing number of Christian women who aren't about to stop working—and they're not apologizing for it. *I work because I have to provide for my family. I love my work yet remain devoted to my family. Working outside my home has made my kids independent and well adjusted. Why can't I serve God at home and at work?*

There are no easy answers.

I went to law school because I had a passion for truth and justice. Sure, I knew I wanted to have a family someday, but that was years and years down the road. For now, I could study hard, make good grades, and land the job of my dreams (or at least make enough money to pay off my student loans). Even though motherhood was a long way away, deep down, I still wondered. *Can I really have it all? Am I going to go through all this schooling, have babies, and put my career on hold?*

For many women, by the time we complete our education and settle into a career, we're smack dab in the middle of our childbearing years. Like it or not, our biological clocks are ticking. Okay, mine wasn't ticking that loudly, but that still didn't stop me from wondering whether I could be an excellent lawyer *and* an excellent mother. After all, I grew up in a traditional home where my devout Christian mother stayed at home. Could I work full time and show the same devotion to my own children? Would the Christian community accept me as a working professional?

The questions continue to burn in the hearts and minds of many young Christian women I meet. Too many women of faith feel like it's either/or: either I am going to serve God and be fully committed to my family *or* I am going to pursue my career with passion and zeal.

Proverbs 31 gives us some answers. No, it doesn't give us *easy* answers, and it doesn't give us a formula. But the woman in Proverbs 31 shows us it's possible to be completely and totally passionate about our family and our work. I have yet to find a stronger role model for modern women.

A WOMAN WHO BREAKS ALL STEREOTYPES

The woman in Proverbs 31 breaks every stereotype I know. As a wife, mother, entrepreneur, trader, and property owner, she's ahead of her time by a few thousand years. She's constantly on the move—both inside and outside of her home. She's clearly a devoted wife and mother—her children bless her and her husband praises her. Yet, in addition to managing her household (and managing it well), she excels in wisdom and instruction, feeds the poor, and runs multiple businesses. All in a day's work!

From the text, it appears she makes linen and garments. But she's not just clothing her family. She selects the finest wool and flax, she works with her hands, and she supplies the merchants with high-quality products. She's obviously a designer with an eye for high fashion. She doesn't just know the latest trend; she sets the latest trend. Her items are highly sought—she produces both quality and quantity, and the merchants keep coming back for more.

But she doesn't stop there. She doesn't just supply and trade high-quality goods. She runs a business. She turns a profit. And then she invests her earnings and opens a new business.

> She considers a field and buys it;
> out of her earnings she plants a vineyard.[1]

In other words, when her garment and trading business becomes profitable, she looks for new ways to expand her resources. So she buys a field. And she doesn't let the field sit empty—she works the field and plants a vineyard. And the vineyard is likely used to raise grapes and turn a healthy profit.

This woman is a true entrepreneur. I get motivated (and tired!) just watching her. She can't possibly run all these businesses by herself—she obviously has to delegate. Perhaps she runs a family business—with her children working in the fields and her husband balancing the books. She's clearly the CEO, and her family is fully supportive.

I'm sure there were days when her children said, *Mommy, do you have to go to the market today? Why can't you play with us?*

I'm sure there were days when her husband said, *Honey, you've really taken on too much. I know you got a really good deal on this new vineyard, but aren't you spread a bit thin?*

And I'm sure there were days when she said to herself, *I just can't do it anymore. I have too many balls in the air and I think I'm going to crack!*

Yet at the end of the day, she is blessed. And in the process, she breaks the stereotypes about wives, mothers, business owners, and women of faith.

THE POWER LAWYER STEREOTYPE

While I'm all for taking a hard look at our decisions involving family and career, common stereotypes can draw unnecessary lines in the sand. I know these stereotypes all too well.

First, there's the stereotype that says I can't be both a high-powered lawyer and a devoted mother. I experience this stereotype firsthand—like when I pick up my daughter from school and another mother starts cross-examining me about my job. We have met once or twice, and she doesn't realize I am a lawyer until my daughter (then age six) apparently announces my occupation to the class.

After explaining to her where I work, she wants to know why I work for a large law firm, why I don't work part time, and why part time isn't an option. And she genuinely feels sorry for me.

"You poor thing. You must work all the time."

Mind you, I don't believe this woman is judging me. (Usually the judgmental conversations are much more subtle, and she is candid and quite sincere.) She just appears confused and genuinely concerned—that I must live a terribly conflicted life.

THE CHURCH LADY STEREOTYPE

The second stereotype I experience is just as bad. Like when I'm speaking to a client I've represented in contentious litigation. He knows me as a tough lawyer, not as someone who writes working mom blogs and faith-based books. When he learns that I'm more than a hired gun (and I actually have a soul outside of the courtroom), he stares at me in disbelief.

"I never thought you would be *that* type."

Am I supposed to take that as a compliment? Maybe I'm not doing a very good job of representing Jesus in the workplace. Or maybe he thinks that faith and work don't belong in the same sentence—that I can't possibly bring my faith to work unless I am weak and powerless. Whatever the case, I know that I don't fit his stereotype. Power lawyer and church lady just don't mesh.

When I feel the weight of these stereotypes, I reach one conclusion. I want to be more like the woman in Proverbs 31.

I don't think she sits around worrying about what people think. Frankly, she doesn't have the time! She is too busy living life to the fullest to worry about whether she "fits" a certain mold. The men in the marketplace and the workers in her vineyard are likely surprised that she is both tough in business and soft at home, but the quality of her work speaks for itself. One of the first things I notice about this woman is her unapologetic pursuit of excellence in every area of her life.

The Pursuit of Excellence—Not Perfection

Back to the question, is it really possible to have it all? Proverbs 31 shows us that it is possible—even desirable—to pursue excellence both at home and at work. But excellence is not perfection. And too often we confuse the two.

Perfection drives us to a zero-sum game and puts the focus on our achievement rather than our character. It's all about us—what we can accomplish to stack our resumes, build our networks, and reward our hard work. It's about giving our families the best of everything—the best resources, the best communities, the best schools. And we can spend every minute of the day striving to make everything line up. The only problem? Who decides where to cut corners?

After all, we only have so many resources—our time, money, and talent. When we use our resources in one area of life, another area will logically suffer the consequences. If we spend more time at work, we lose precious time at home. If we go back to school and further our education, we might lose opportunities at work. It we want to donate time, we may make less money. If we want to earn more money, we may have less time. The pie is only so big. If perfection is the goal, how do we decide to slice the pie, and who will get the smallest piece?

The Zero Sum Game in Action

After I had my firstborn, Nick, I wanted to be the perfect mother. Sure, I knew deep down that perfection wasn't achievable, but like many new mothers I wanted to do my best. This pursuit of perfection manifested itself shortly after I returned to work. Because it was time away from Nick, I felt like I couldn't take a lunch. My rationale went something like this. *If I take an hour for lunch, I'll end up working an hour later every day. Then, I'll see Nick for an hour less each day. Taking lunch is selfish. If I work through lunch, I am making a sacrifice for Nick, and I'm a better mother in the process.*

This didn't stop at lunch. The zero-sum mentality made me feel like I had to prioritize every task—to determine its value—before investing time. Things like taking a walk or meeting a friend for coffee quickly felt selfish and unimportant. After all, if I was going to be the "best" mother I could be and work outside my home, I had to cut everything else that wasn't vital to my family.

Of course, this type of perfectionism isn't sustainable. If we read Proverbs 31 and walk away thinking perfectionism is the goal, we will be sorely disappointed. We know all too well that the perfect kids, perfect marriage, and perfect job don't exist. Yet Proverbs 31 describes a woman of noble character, not a perfectionist. Proverbs 31 isn't about perfection. It's about excellence.

Putting Our Talents on the Table

Excellence is still worth pursuing. In Proverbs 31, the woman's garments are sought after because she has high standards—she works hard to put out a high-quality product. And she loses some sleep in the process. She "gets up while it is still dark" and "her lamp does not go out at night."[2] She knows that pursuing excellence involves sacrifice. Most days, she is probably exhausted. She knows what it means to burn the candle at both ends and not have enough hours in the day. No, it's not a perfect existence, but it allows her to pursue her passions. Many nights, she finishes her work while her family is sleeping. But lack of sleep and limited resources don't hold her back. At the end of the day, she gets it done and she gets it done well.

In pursuing her passions, she doesn't wonder, "What if?" She strives to put all of her talents on the table. In the words of Erma Bombeck, she is emptying herself of talent in the hope of achieving a greater good.

> When I stand before God at the end of my life, I would hope that I would not have a single bit of talent left, and could say, 'I used everything you gave me.'[3]

These words ring true to a woman who is living life to the fullest. Pursuing excellence means putting all of our talents on the table. Not wondering, what if? And not being limited by stereotypes and culture. It means using what God gives us and leaving the results to him. It means saying good-bye to perfection.

The Pursuit of Integration—Not Juggling

Yet perfection isn't our only battle. Even if we've kissed perfection good-bye, no one said it would be easy. Excellence is hard work. And, more often than not, we find ourselves in a constant war of apparently conflicting roles, also called the juggling act. Working women are constantly switching gears. There are too many balls to drop. Too many hats to wear. Too many people to please.

When I look at the woman in Proverbs 31, she doesn't seem to constantly switch roles. She doesn't stop being a mom and wife when she buys a field and plants a vineyard. She lives a life of integration—not constant juggling—and she merges what we too often see as competing worlds.

She doesn't apologize for who she is. She doesn't apologize for who she isn't. She doesn't muzzle her children while she's on conference calls or pretend that she's "at a meeting" when she's really at the ball field. Likewise, she doesn't hesitate to leave work early when her children are sick, and she reschedules a client meeting around her daughter's birthday party.

We have so much to learn from this woman.

I used to think of my life as a juggling act. Juggling a full-time job, three kids, a spouse, and extended family and friends (not to mention hobbies and pets) involves lots of balls. But sometimes, I run out of hands. I've even been known to drop a few balls in midair.

Which is where the blender comes in. Forget juggling. I just throw it all into the same bowl and turn on the switch. There are three speeds: low, medium, and high. I usually run on medium, and I save high for when I really need it. Like when I'm up all night with a sick kid the evening before a big deadline at work and gear myself up to live on heavy doses of prayer and caffeine. Yet in these moments of chaos, I've learned I'm at my best when I abandon the juggling act and just turn on the blender.

IS BALANCE OUT?

In a world of technology, social media, and careers that demand nothing less than a chunk of our flesh, it's no longer realistic to compartmentalize. The days of "my time" are over (I'm not sure they ever even existed for most women). Every attempt to draw a line in the sand backfires. So, as much as I try to separate my personal life from my professional life, I've learned by necessity just to blend them together.

How does this play out in real life? For many working women, our work spills into our homes. We get calls at home late at night, usually when it's inconvenient. Our cell phones ring in the pediatrician's office. We bring our laptops on vacation. But the opposite is also true. The pediatrician always calls us at the office. We work at home when our kids are sick. Maybe we even take our entire family on a business trip and turn it into a vacation.

Some would accuse us of lacking balance. My response? Balance is out. Blenders are in. Why fight it? I'm not saying it's right or wrong. For many of us, it's just the way it is. I'm tired of changing my cape every time I switch from home to work and work to home. And I don't see the woman in Proverbs 31 constantly flipping the switch. I'm a passionate mother *and* a passionate lawyer. Can't I be both at the same time? Or do I need to take great pains to compartmentalize my life so that no one can ever discover the real me?

I'm not saying that the blender is for everyone. It raises lots of issues, like—*Is anyone really getting my undivided attention?* I'm also not saying that Proverbs 31 teaches us to work 24/7 and abandon all boundaries. It was likely easier to lead an integrated life before the invention of email, iPhones, and social media. If the woman of Proverbs 31 saw our lifestyles, she would probably tell us to slow down. But I don't think she'd tell us to compartmentalize either.

At the end of the day, an integrated life can be freeing. For me, the blender allows me to be who I am without having to choose among multiple worlds. It's a far cry from perfect, but it feels authentic. It allows me to be me—the person God created.

The Pursuit of God—Not Beauty and Charm

We can't walk away from Proverbs 31 without noticing the most important quality about this woman. Her character. Otherwise, the Proverbs 31 message becomes, *Nobody's perfect and be yourself. And while you're at it, get a blender.*

While this message has value, it's also wholly inadequate. Something is missing. Character is what makes this woman different. Not the fact that she is turning a profit, running multiple businesses, and managing a successful family. Her true mark of greatness is her heart—not her pocket book or even the approval of her family.

As a woman of noble character, she opens her arms to the poor, maintains a sense of humor, and is full of wisdom and instruction—in addition to being a devoted wife and mother. Such a woman is a rare find—"A wife of noble *character*, who can find?"[4] She's the kind of woman we all want to honor.

So what's her secret? The end of the chapter tells us: "Charm is deceitful and beauty is vain, but a woman who fears the LORD, she shall be praised."[5]

In other words, this woman isn't obsessed with appearances. She knows that charm and manipulation might win a battle or two, but it will never win the war. She knows that outward beauty will never sustain a relationship. She knows that the people who judge her by her beauty will eventually lose interest and move on.

She instead focuses on the one relationship that is never based on appearances: her relationship with God. In fearing the Lord, she places inner beauty over outward beauty. She knows that this earthly shell is fleeting, and while society continues to judge women on the outside, God will always value our hearts.

⁂

Thousands of years later, we're still struggling to be women of noble character. It's still a tough road. Yet Proverbs 31 shows us that it's possible. We too can pursue lives of excellence and integration and not obsess over what people think. We too can focus on inward beauty and resist the pressures of perfection and appearances. And we too can focus on the one relationship that will measure our success by the quality of our character, not by the list of our achievements.

Are you ready to be a Proverbs 31 woman?

Questions for Chapter Nine

1. What are some of the stereotypes about working women today in the church? What are some of the stereotypes in the professional world about women in the church? How does Proverbs 31 speak to both of these stereotypes?

2. Have you ever confused excellence and perfection? Do you agree that perfectionism can lead to the zero-sum game?

3. Is it possible to "have it all"? Is balance even a worthy goal?

4. What can we learn from the character traits set forth in Proverbs 31?

ۑ *Select readings:* Proverbs 31

CHAPTER NINE NOTES

1. Proverbs 31:16.
2. Proverbs 31:15, 18.
3. Erma Bombeck, (U.S. humorist, 1927-1996).
4. Proverbs 31:10 (emphasis mine).
5. Proverbs 31:30 (NASB).

Chapter Ten

MARY

Moving toward the Pain

When I first wrote this book, Mary didn't make the cut. Simply put, I was reluctant to write about her. So much has already been said. More books have been written about Mary than any other woman of the Bible. More pictures have been painted, more songs have been composed, and more drama has been played about this one woman.

Yet I couldn't bring myself to leave her out.

It all started when my son scolded me for the omission. He was beyond perplexed when I admitted under heavy cross-examination that a book about the working women of the Bible didn't include Mary. "Mom, isn't the mother of Jesus the most important working woman in the Bible?" he asked with indignation.

It's a fair question. A question that caused me to think deeply about Mary's lifework. What kind of woman does it take to raise the Son of God?

Raising kids is hard work for any mother. In fact, most mothers find it to be the most rewarding yet most difficult work we do. While I've always worked outside the home, I know better than to think the life of a stay-at-home mom is any "easier." All mothers work, and we carry heavy hearts shouldering the physical, emotional, and spiritual needs of our children at every age and stage of the journey. Every mother is wrestling with some unattainable standard of perfection.

Mary is no stranger to the Superwoman complex. In fact, all working women can learn greatly from Mary's approach to work and her uncanny ability to handle pressure. Raising God's Son involves more pressure than we will ever know, at home or at work!

WANTED: THE MOTHER OF GOD

What kind of woman is cut out for this seemingly divine task? If a want ad appeared online for the Mother of God, what would it look like?

> *Wanted. Devoted mother to raise the Son of God. Requirements include advanced degrees in psychology and theology, impeccable reputation, stable marriage, and experience raising multiple children in loving home. Strong references required.*

Position, experience, and resources are at the top of the list. The mother of God is going to have a difficult job—maybe the hardest job ever—and she needs every earthly advantage. It's not easy to find the right caregiver. I'd like to think that God can relate to the millions of working mothers who diligently seek out the best child care for their children! He scours the earth to find Mary. Yet on first blush his choice is surprising—Mary doesn't appear ready or qualified.

Mary is likely a young teenager when she is asked to take on this enormous job. She is not yet a mother. She is unmarried. She is poor and uneducated. And her reputation is about to be tarnished forever. As soon as she becomes pregnant out of wedlock she will face public ridicule and shame. Her betrothed will likely leave her alone to raise the child. No one will give her a reference let alone exalt her credentials as a caregiver, wife, or mother. Based on human standards, she will never get the job. Yet God still conducts an interview. Without warning.

She is completely unprepared. Maybe that's the point.

A Job Interview with an Angel

Most of us like to prepare for an important job interview. We extensively research the background of the potential employer. We want to know who will be conducting the interview so we can run a Google search and check the LinkedIn profile. We anticipate the questions that will be asked. We plan for a good breakfast, show up early, and put our best foot forward.

Mary doesn't have any time to prepare. She doesn't have a typical job interview. It's not as if she submits her resume or answers an ad to be the mother of God. In fact, she doesn't do anything. She is just available.

Mary is likely minding her own business when she is blindsided by the angel Gabriel. Gabriel is God's delegate and recruitment coordinator. (No, he's not on LinkedIn, and he doesn't even give Mary the courtesy of a knock.)

The angel went to her and said, "Greetings, you who are highly favored! The Lord is with you."

Mary was greatly troubled at his words and wondered what kind of greeting this might be. But the angel said to her, "Do not be afraid, Mary; you have found favor with God. You will conceive and give birth to a son, and you are to call him Jesus. He will be great and will be called the Son of the Most High. The Lord God will give him the throne of his father David, and he will reign over Jacob's descendants forever; his kingdom will never end."

"How will this be," Mary asked the angel, "since I am a virgin?"

The angel answered, "The Holy Spirit will come on you, and the power of the Most High will overshadow you. So the holy one to be born will be called the Son of God. Even Elizabeth your relative is going to have a child in her old age, and she who was said to be unable to conceive is in her sixth month. For no word from God will ever fail."

"I am the Lord's servant," Mary answered. "May your word to me be fulfilled." Then the angel left her.[1]

This could be the most important and most terrifying job interview in all of history.

Gabriel doesn't come with a list of questions. Like I said, nothing about this interview is typical. He doesn't challenge her credentials—in fact, he repeatedly affirms her with God's favor.

Mary isn't completely silent. She may be in shock, but she still has the courage to ask a legitimate and practical question: *how* in the world will this happen since she in a virgin?

Gabriel speaks with both brevity and certainty. The Holy Spirit will impregnate her. She may not understand, but she is willing. Mary's response is overwhelming. She just says yes.

SAYING YES TO GOD

"I am the Lord's servant."

It's really that simple. She doesn't ask a bunch of questions about what, where, and when. She doesn't even hesitate. She sees the opportunity of a lifetime and she takes it. Sure she has more questions, but she is still prepared to act.

When I contrast Mary's interview with my own agenda, I notice stark differences. I am always trying to build my resume. I anticipate and worry about what's next. Will I miss God's will if I don't seek out the right opportunities at the right time? Will I even hear God if he calls? After all, I don't want to miss something "important." What actions should *I* be taking *right now* to make sure my future is secure?

Yet Mary shows us we overestimate our plans. We underestimate the power of simply being available. Mary may not be seeking out her position, but God knows where to find her. He's an expert in the recruiting business. He's been watching Mary for years. In fact, he knew her before she was born. This isn't just about Mary. God is ready.

Mary's response to this unconventional and terrifying interview gives new meaning to the phrase *attitude is everything*. How many times have we said in our work, "Just tell me what to do, I'll get it done!"

LETTING GO OF THE FIVE-YEAR PLAN

When Mary says yes, she is letting go of every plan she ever had about her future. This is a woman who planned to marry a carpenter. She planned to be surrounded by family and friends and lead a boring life. Mary doesn't strike me as the type of woman who wanted attention, stress, and drama. Yet her five-year plan of a couple of kids and a quiet home with Joseph is turned upside down.

God has other plans.

Mary is about to become an outcast among her own friends and family. While Joseph will support her, she will have no relatives or friends to help her birth and care for her newborn during those first exhausting and exhilarating months of Jesus' life. I firmly believe God provided her cousin Elizabeth as a mentor,[2] but going solo with your firstborn isn't exactly what most mothers envision about childbirth. Not to mention the barbaric and filthy quarters of a stable. Forget birthing coaches and drugs, Mary simply had to survive.

Mary has us in awe and wonder.

> Every Christmas, when I get out the familiar
> nativity scene, I stop for a moment and hold Mary
> in my hand. I wonder if childbirth was exhil-
> arating for her, or whether she was too scared

and unprepared to enjoy the moment. . . . I can't
wait to ask her someday what it was like to birth
Jesus in a stable. Where did she get the swaddling
clothes? Did she bring them on the journey, or did
she borrow them from the inn?[3]

She is undoubtedly resourceful. She has to be. The five-year
plan is out the window. She will soon escape to Egypt with
Joseph—another journey she never planned—to hide Jesus from
the authorities and save his life. She is again away from extended
family and alone with Joseph—yet they are in this together. They
are fully committed to their life's work of protecting and raising
Jesus. No one said it was going to be easy.

A Single Working Mother

Sometime between Jesus' twelfth and thirty-third birthdays,
Mary becomes a single mother. While many have speculated
about the timing of Joseph's death, we simply don't know
whether Jesus had an earthly father during his teenage years
and into manhood. Joseph is still alive when Jesus is age twelve,
based on the account in Luke chapter 2. When Jesus begins his
public ministry at age thirty, Joseph is absent. By the time of
Jesus' death three years later, Joseph has clearly left the scene.[4]

Clearly, losing Joseph isn't part of Mary's plan. Joseph is the
only person who knows the truth about Jesus' birth. He is the
only person she has walked with on this riveting and mysterious
journey. He is the only person who understands. How can God
take him away when Mary needs him more than ever? How will
she endure the pain that lies ahead?

Yet Mary rises to the occasion with grace and mercy. No wonder so many women—including single working mothers— call her blessed.

When Joseph dies, Mary assumes responsibility as the head of household. It's up to her to put food on the table, wipe the tears of her children, and make sure her home is a place where God is honored. And that's all on top of raising the Son of God! It's too much pressure for one woman to bear.

Her children likewise work to provide for the family. As the oldest child, Jesus is likely the breadwinner as a carpenter (a trade he learned from his father) as well as the source of Mary's comfort. For every mother who is accused of being "Mommy Dearest" or not wanting to let go of her son, Mary can more than relate. Jesus is her rock. He's the reason she gets up in the morning, and he's the last thing she thinks about when she goes to bed. It's all for him, and he makes life as a single working mother worth every moment.

Yet hanging on to Jesus—the very thing that Mary wants and needs to do—is the one thing she can't do. Ever since Jesus was a boy, she has practiced letting go.

LETTING GO OF OUR WORK

Starting with pregnancy and childbirth, Mary has to let go of her expectations. This is a woman who ponders—she doesn't push. She refuses to constantly intervene.

It's after the annual trip to Jerusalem for the Passover. After the feast, Mary and Joseph start to make the journey back home, assuming Jesus is traveling behind with relatives. They travel for a whole day until they realize he isn't with them!

Can you imagine how terrible they must have felt? *God, I'm sorry about the mix-up, but it appears that we have lost your one and only Son.*

It's the ancient story of *Home Alone.* And it's not difficult to imagine. After all, Jesus is twelve years old—almost a man. It's not like he's a naughty boy or a rebellious child. He has never disobeyed his parents. Not once. And they probably think he is hanging out with his cousins. Mary probably thought, *Of course I don't have to worry about him. He is with family!*

So Mary and Joseph completely lose track. Once they realize Jesus is gone, they head back to Jerusalem and search for three whole days (and probably a couple of sleepless nights). Finally, they find Jesus in the temple.[5]

No doubt it's a traumatic experience for Mary. So what does she do? Did she lock Jesus up? Did she forbid him to ever leave home again?

To the extent Mary wants to be in control, she must let go. To the extent she wants to worry, she must relinquish.

UNDERSTANDING IS NOT A PREREQUISITE

How does she get to this place of letting go? She must have understood God's plan. God must have given her special insight and assurances about the future. Right?

Wrong. Understanding is not a prerequisite to Mary's actions.

Luke chapter 2 tells us two things: (1) she "did not understand" Jesus' actions (v. 50) and (2) she "treasured all these things in her heart" (v. 51).

In other words, she doesn't freak out, even though she lacks understanding about the future. And while she ponders things deeply, she doesn't overreact.

We know that Mary's heart is constantly full of quiet emotion. From the day that Jesus is born, she is filled with contemplation. Like when the shepherds come to worship Jesus, everyone is amazed and excited. "But Mary treasured up all these things and pondered them in her heart" (Luke 2:19).

What's the difference between worry and ponder? Worry is focused on what we can't do to change the circumstances. Ponder is watching what God does through the circumstances. Worry pushes the panic button. Ponder takes a deep breath and waits. Worry intervenes. Ponder lets go even when we don't understand.

INFLUENCING OUR WORK

Mary shows us that letting go doesn't mean giving up our influence. In fact, it frequently involves exerting our influence. Notice how she quietly yet firmly nudges Jesus to perform his first miracle.

> When the wine was gone, Jesus' mother said to him,
> "They have no more wine."
> "Dear woman, why do you involve me?" Jesus replied.
> "My time has not yet come."
> His mother said to the servants, "Do whatever he tells you."[6]

Mary is so subtle that it's easy to miss her action. She has known for years that Jesus is no ordinary son—for thirty years. She has held Jesus in her arms and watched him grow. She has watched him toil in a carpenter shop supporting the family. She has seen God at work to mold him into a man. And she can now see that Jesus is ready.

If she nudges him now, she may lose him. She may not be ready, but she still acts.

Mary gives Jesus a nudge. A gentle nudge. She knows that God has a greater plan—a plan that she committed to execute during that first interview with Gabriel.

Notice the strength of this nudge. Mary is both patient and deliberate. She's not overbearing. She doesn't say, *Jesus, if you're ever going to be anything special you better hurry up. Time is running out. You're going to be past your prime!*

No, she simply presents an opportunity. She doesn't act for him. In nudging Jesus, she tells him, *Look, I'll be okay. I know you have bigger and better things to do—please don't let me hold you back.* She allows God to act.

She makes it look so easy!

Too often, we think that influence is won by force. Or at least by being bossy. But Mary gets it done with a nudge. A quiet and thoughtful nudge.

MOVING TOWARD THE PAIN

In nudging Jesus to act, Mary doesn't move toward her own plans or ideas. She moves toward pain.

Think about it. Mary is urging her son to reveal his true identity and embrace his life's work. This will come at great cost. Jesus is the breadwinner who puts food on her table. Since

Joseph has died, he's the only one who understands. Is she ready for him to move out and move on?

Of course not. Letting go of Jesus at his first public miracle is only the beginning of her pain. She has raised the Son of God as a widow. She has high hopes and dreams for his future—maybe he will save the nation and become king. She goes on to watch him launch a "failed" ministry. She helplessly stands by and watches him suffer and die on a cross.

I can't imagine more painful work.

Sure, it must have been exhilarating when Jesus rose from the dead, but don't think that took away Mary's pain. When the risen Jesus reveals himself to Mary, he is not there to stay. He is there to say good-bye.

Can she really lose him again?

At this point, I don't know whether Mary understands her life's work. Certainly, she doesn't fully understand the reason for her pain. It's easy for us to say, "Well, of course she rises to the occasion. She is the mother of God!"

But Mary doesn't feel like a celebrity. She feels pain, confusion, and even doubt. Yet she presses on and fulfills her promise to the angel.

"I am the Lord's servant."

Through her pain, she blesses us for generations and generations to come. She shows us that sometimes we need to move toward the pain to achieve something divine.

Discussion Questions for Chapter Ten

1. How do Mary's "credentials" uniquely qualify her to be the mother of Jesus?

2. Have you ever thought of Mary as a single mother? Does this help to appreciate the pressure and stress she must have encountered?

3. Mary says yes to God, even though she lacks information and understanding. How does her attitude change our approach to daily work?

4. Does greater pain lead to greater accomplishments in our work? Can you think of any examples?

ટ *Select readings:* Luke chapters 1 and 2

CHAPTER TEN NOTES

1. Luke 1:28–38.

2. Susan DiMickele, *Chasing Superwoman* (Colorado Springs, CO: Cook, 2010), 52. I had read the story of Mary and Elizabeth since I was a child but only recently was struck by God's complete brilliance in using the birth of John the Baptist to prepare Mary for her own labor and delivery. When the angel Gabriel visited Mary and foretold the birth of Christ, Elizabeth—John the Baptist's mother-to-be—was already six months pregnant. Mary went to visit Elizabeth and stayed with her three months. Six plus three is nine, so Mary must have stayed for John's birth. Assuming she did, she would have watched and learned about labor and delivery first-hand from her older cousin Elizabeth.

3. Ibid., 53.

4. As Jesus is on the cross, he squarely asks the Apostle John to care for Mary as his own mother. John 19:26–27.

5. Luke 2:41–52.

6. John 2:3–5.

Chapter Eleven

MARTHA
The Workaholic

was feeling pretty sorry for myself on Easter morning. I stayed up late Saturday night filling Easter baskets and hiding eggs. I got up early Sunday morning to make everyone breakfast, and I ran around like a chicken with my head cut off to make sure we were ready for church by 9:00 a.m. As I rushed the family out to the car, I screamed at my husband, "Why don't you help me? Can't you see that I can't do it all?"

My tantrum on Easter morning isn't all that unusual. As women, we often feel like we have to do it all—and we love to complain about it. In addition to our jobs, we're often responsible for planning schedules, making meals, volunteering for every bake sale and fundraiser, and pulling off every holiday and birthday—as well as shouldering the social and spiritual development of our families. We tell ourselves, *I never signed up for this pressure. When did life become so complicated?*

Sometimes, the physical, emotional, and spiritual needs of our families are too much for us to handle. We look around us, and we can't find a shortcut. The women around us have the same struggles, the same schedules, and the same pressures.

Martha of Bethany understands. She may have lived over two thousand years ago, but she struggles with the same fundamental dilemma as you and I. Her story sounds all too familiar. Her cry is universal,

Jesus, why do I have to do it all?

A Leader, Not a Follower

The first time we meet Martha,[1] we notice she is a leader, not a follower. She has resources, opinions, and influence.

First and foremost, she owns her own home. This means she has financial independence, inheritance, or both. Martha is likely a single working woman. She may be a widow. She may be saddled with so many family responsibilities—like taking care of her younger brother and sister and putting food on the table—that she simply doesn't have time for a family of her own.

Being an older sibling and head of household is part of her identity. Martha takes care of the family. The family doesn't take care of Martha. In fact, no one is taking care of Martha—or, at least she certainly feels that way. And it feels pretty lonely on her own.

Like many of us, Martha tells God, *Lord, if I don't do it, it's not going to get done.* She's the one who brings home the bacon. She's the one who stocks the refrigerator and prepares the meals. She's the one who gets up early to make sure the clothes are washed and stays up late to balance the checkbook.

THE ULTIMATE HOSTESS

Martha does it all. All the time. She doesn't sit back and wait for the action. Instead, she finds the action and gets involved. Notice how she takes the initiative to open her home to Jesus.

> As Jesus and his disciples were on their way, he came to a village where a woman named Martha opened her home to him.[2]

It doesn't say that a family opened their home to Jesus. It doesn't say that Martha, Mary, and Lazarus opened their home to Jesus. It says that Martha opened her home to Jesus.

In other words, Martha is the host. The dinner party is her idea. Martha is the kind of woman who opens up her home on a regular basis. Not only does she host, but she has the perfect invitations and finest food, not to mention matching napkins and clever favors. She thinks of everything. And her thoughtfulness doesn't end at home. She's the kind of friend who offers to pick your kid up at baseball when you're running late. She brings you an extra set of forms when you miss the meeting at work. And she never forgets to send you a birthday card.

We all need a friend like Martha. And we all admire her capacity to get everything done and get it done well. On the outside, she looks like she has it all together. We wish we had half her energy. *I don't know how she does it. She never tires.* But on the inside, Martha is struggling. Sure, she may look like she has it all together, but if she puts one more thing on her plate, she is going to crack. Who has time for Jesus when there's too much work to be done?

MISSING JESUS IN THE MIDDLE OF THE LIVING ROOM

By definition, *doing it all* is both exhausting and impossible. Like too many women, Martha is so consumed with activity—throwing dinner parties, running errands, taking on a new project at work—that she can't be still. Martha doesn't have enough hours in the day.

Imagine the stress of having the Son of God as her dinner guest. Should she serve white wine or red wine? Or no wine? How many people are going to show up? How much food should she prepare, and what if she doesn't have enough?

Naturally, Martha wants everything to be perfect. The dinner party is a reflection of her. So, she tries hard to impress everyone—especially Jesus. After all, she's doing this all for him. Martha is "distracted by all the preparations that had to be made."[3] Throwing together the perfect dinner party for Jesus is no simple task. Especially with substandard help—or, in the case of her sister Mary, no help at all!

Who isn't distracted these days, and why are we picking on Martha? What's wrong with being overly productive? Someone has to throw a dinner party for Jesus. Someone has to be in charge. If not her, then who? Isn't her work a noble task?

Martha's work is noble indeed. Which makes her plight all the more frustrating. In doing noble work, Martha misses what's most important. She puts the party ahead of Jesus. She puts what she is doing for Jesus ahead of Jesus himself.

Jesus is sitting in Martha's living room and she doesn't even see him. Talk about distracted!

Life Just Isn't Fair

Not only is she distracted, Martha has a bit of a tantrum in the middle of her dinner party. Like my tantrum on Easter morning, she stomps her feet and pounds her fists. She doesn't have a husband to complain to, so she whines to Jesus, *Lord, don't you care that my sister has left me to do the work by myself? Tell her to help me* (Luke 10:40)!

So much for honoring the dinner guest. She all but blames him for her plight—and throws her sister under the bus in the process. In front of a whole room of guests! We've all been to a party when the host comes unglued. It can be pretty awkward.

Obviously, this is about more than a dinner party. Martha is carrying some resentment. She doesn't think life is fair. And she's right. It's not. Martha is tired of being the responsible older sister. She's tired of holding it all together. And in this case, she is slaving away in the kitchen—all for Jesus—yet he doesn't even notice. Talk about unfair. Mary the slacker is doing nothing and getting all his attention.

But Jesus isn't impressed. He gets right to the point.

"You are worried and upset about many things, but only one thing is needed."[4]

He further instructs Martha that "Mary has chosen what it better."[5]

The nerve of him. Does he have to throw salt on the wound?

Jesus could have told Martha, *I'm so sorry, Martha. I know life isn't fair. You have to do all the work. Please be patient with your younger sister. It's really thoughtful of you to serve in the kitchen—we all really appreciate your hard work.*

But he doesn't placate her. Instead, he speaks truth in love. He tells her to get over herself.

MARTHA'S WORK IS NOT THE PROBLEM

I used to think Martha just needed to slow down. Work smarter, not harder. Go to the spa for a day. Learn to set boundaries and just say no. If Martha was in our midst today, we'd tell her to get a job coach, learn to delegate, and take some time for herself. But while all of these coping skills might help for a time, they wouldn't solve Martha's dilemma. Martha's work is not the problem.

Something bigger is in play.

The problem isn't work itself. The problem is how Martha views work. Most of us can relate to one (or more) of her symptoms.

- Martha is a multitaskaholic.
- Martha is working for significance.
- Martha is carrying her own load—and it's too heavy.

The Martha syndrome is all too familiar.

Symptom #1: Being a Multitaskaholic

It's difficult to focus when you're doing twenty things at once. No wonder Martha is distracted. She's what we call a multitaskaholic.

Many of us suffer from this symptom. Even though we claim to be multitasking, research shows that our brains can't focus on more than one thing at a time. And Martha is no different. She is focused on an important task at the moment—pulling off the perfect dinner party for Jesus. Who could blame her for being a little preoccupied?

Emotionally Absent

Here's the problem. Martha may be physically present, but she's not emotionally present. Her work is crowding out her most important relationships. No doubt, she is working for everyone around her. But there's only so much of Martha to go around.

Martha doesn't even have a mobile phone or laptop to distract her. Imagine Martha with twenty-first-century technology. Or Martha gone wild on Facebook. Would she ever unplug?

Technology has a way of gripping our attention and not letting go. I've officially been diagnosed as a multitaskaholic. I can't help but pull out my iPhone when I'm sitting at dinner with my husband. I tell him I'm just "checking on the kids," but I find myself absorbed by the latest drama at work. No wonder he calls my iPhone my "second husband." I've stopped short of bringing my mobile devices into church—the only hour of the week where I am truly unplugged. But when I exit, the first thing I do is check my messages—never mind focusing on the service or having a moment of reflection. I've missed a whole hour of email traffic and texting.

And I'm not alone. I notice other parents at the soccer games, sitting on their smart phones and surfing the net while their unruly younger children sit next to them playing hand-held video games. We're not only a distracted generation—we're raising the next generation to view multitasking as the norm. The TV is on while we're eating breakfast; we're on a conference call as we rush to a doctor's appointment; we leave a meeting early to get to another meeting late.

Distracted or Devoted?

I wonder, what would the research show about distracted workers? Are we more likely to make sloppy mistakes? Are we more likely to be disconnected from our co-workers? Do others around us feel undervalued and neglected? Like distracted drivers, are we more likely to crash?

Jesus sees right through Martha's busyness. Her distractions are compromising her devotion, and he wants her full attention.

Too many of us can relate. When's the last time we gave anyone or anything our full attention? When's the last time we put down our smart phones for a day and sat at the feet of Jesus?

Symptom #2: Martha Is Working for Significance

Martha isn't just distracted; she is trying to work her way to Jesus. She thinks her performance earns favor with God. If she serves Jesus and serves him well, he will see how much she loves him. If she is good enough, maybe he will accept her. It's all up to Martha to get it right—with the Son of God as her audience, the pressure is on. She doesn't want to make a mistake or disappoint him.

Martha is a workaholic. And, in the process of working so hard to get it right, she forgets that Jesus first wants her heart. Her work can follow.

How many workaholics say, "I'm doing it all for my family" or even, "I'm working for God alone." Yet who are we really working for? What are we trying to prove?

The Humility of a "Sinner"

Contrast Martha with Mary. While Martha is working, Mary is sitting. Mary probably doesn't know what it's like to hold a steady job or earn an honest living. She's never been the leader in the home or the responsible one. And she knows what it's like to need complete and total forgiveness.

In Luke 7 we read about a woman who washes Jesus' feet with her tears.

> When a woman who had lived a sinful life in that town learned that Jesus was eating at the Pharisee's house, she brought an alabaster jar of perfume, and as she stood behind him at his feet weeping, she began to wet his feet with her tears.[6]

The Pharisees are disturbed at this outrageous conduct, but Jesus rises to her defense.

> "'Therefore, I tell you, her many sins have been forgiven—for she loved much. But he who has been forgiven little loves little.'"[7]

When the disciple John later refers to Mary he explains, "This Mary, whose brother Lazarus now lay sick, was the same one who poured perfume on the Lord and wiped his feet with her hair."[8] Is Mary of Bethany the same woman referenced in Luke 7—the women who "lived a sinful life" and wets Jesus' feet with her tears? Most scholars believe this is a different woman and a different occasion.[9] Others aren't sure. We know that Mary of Bethany likewise washes Jesus' feet with perfume. She is likewise a woman who loves much and is forgiven much. She has the humility of a sinner.

Jesus changes Mary by giving her new life. He gives her hope and forgiveness. A clean slate. A chance to be worthy despite her performance. She can't help but sit at his feet.

Could it be that Martha is a bit embarrassed by her sister? That she can't forget the scars of Mary's sinful past? As Mary sits at Jesus' feet, she is showing a lapse of judgment. Will she ever learn? She's sitting in a room full of men—in a questionable position—when she should be in the kitchen with her sister. Mary is risking her reputation (and the reputation of her family) by breaking a cultural norm in the middle of their living room.

Yet Jesus isn't hung up on what people think. Instead, he sees Mary seeking him with her whole heart. His work is her work. Dinner can wait. Jesus is in her midst, and she finds her significance in who he is, not in what she's done.

Provocative Grace

Many of us, like Martha, can't wrap our heads around Mary's actions. We find significance in what we do. We think we're doing everything right—and that God needs us to throw that dinner party. We look down on those who do less "important" work. And while our contributions may be meaningful, we lack humility. Like Martha, we are confounded by grace.

Jesus' words to Martha don't just catch us by surprise. They shock us. How can he say Mary has chosen what is better? How can sitting in the living room (in a questionable position) be better than serving the guest of honor? How can lounging around be superior to actually getting something done?

We can't begin to understand. Yet the irony of grace is not what we give but what we are given. The workaholic can't boast.

> For it is by grace you have been saved, through faith—and this is not from yourselves, it is the gift of God—not by works, so that no one can boast."[10]

We don't earn a thing. Grace is God's gift to us, and our work is a gift to God. Those of us trying to earn a promotion with God can stop working ourselves to death. We can breathe a sigh of relief.

Grace is provocative for the workaholic.

Symptom #3: Carrying a (Too) Heavy Load

Not all women are multitaskaholics or workaholics. Yet many of us can relate to the last symptom of the Martha syndrome— carrying a heavy load. We have too much on our plates and not enough hours in the day.

Who else will do it?

Martha is carrying her load alone. And it's just too heavy. Not just physically, but mentally. Martha has to be the strong one. She's dealing with two younger siblings who can't pull their own weight—Mary has a bit of a checkered past, and Lazarus can't step up and be the man of the house. So what option does Martha really have?

The fact of the matter is, most days I carry the weight of the world on my shoulders. If I don't do it, I worry it won't get done.

Who is going to stock the refrigerator?

Who else will arrange for carpool duty?

Who is going to sign my kids up for summer camp? (By the way, I always miss the deadline and have to beg for grace.)

Who else will buy the Christmas gifts, send the birthday cards, and plan the holiday gatherings?

I think it's natural—maybe even healthy—for women to have these struggles. God gives us special insight into our homes. I firmly believe a woman's instinct is something that can't be replicated or delegated. But God doesn't want us to carry our burdens alone.

Not Carrying the Burden Alone

Martha doesn't want to ask for help, but even she gets exasperated. She needs to get over herself, and she has the right idea when she pleads her case to Jesus. Here's Jesus' advice for busy women who do too much:

> "Come to me, all you who are weary and burdened, and I will give you rest. Take my yoke upon you and learn from me, for I am gentle and humble in heart, and you will find rest for your souls."[11]

These words are sugar to my soul. I don't have to do it all myself. Having a God who bears my burdens takes the pressure off me. It takes the pressure off my work. It takes the pressure off my home.

This doesn't mean that the daily grind is any easier (or that we don't need some practical solutions and delegation to divide up the load). But I can't find a "cookie cutter" solution—other than walking by grace each day and learning to "come" when Jesus calls.

Jesus is making an offer worth considering. Like Martha, he's asking us to stop stressing, sit at his feet, and let go.

Should We Just Quit Working?

Does sitting at the feet of Jesus mean giving up on work? Or quitting all together?

We naturally have doubts. How does "letting go" play out in real life? And how does Jesus really view our work?

My work isn't as "important" as planning a dinner party for Jesus. If Jesus isn't impressed with Martha, he's never going to be impressed with me. So how am I supposed to reconcile my work with what's really important?

There's a fine line between doing significant work and putting our significance in work. Like Martha, we may feel like we're earning our way to God. As much as we hate to admit it, our significance is often measured by what we do. And while our work may be very good, it can also be a distraction—especially if we're multitaskaholics or simply carrying (too) heavy loads.

If we suffer from the Martha syndrome, we may feel like throwing in the towel. Why even bother? Especially if our work is pulling us down. Maybe we'd be more spiritual if we decided to hang out in the living room with Mary and never prepare a meal again.

But if we walk away from work we miss the point. We fall into the trap of separating the sacred from the secular. The rationale goes something like this: Mary is sitting at Jesus' feet (sacred) while Martha is preparing dinner (secular). So sitting at Jesus' feet is spiritual. Making dinner is not.

Yet Jesus never applies this logic. He never tells Martha to stop working. He never asks her to apologize for her leadership and skill. Her work is God-given and productive. And while Jesus first wants Martha's heart, he doesn't tell her to quit. He also doesn't tell her to separate her work from her spiritual life. He wants her work to have purpose and meaning.

How do we know that Martha keeps working? When we later read about one of Jesus' last meals with his friends, we see that "Martha served."[12] She thrives in serving Jesus. She's not going to stop. Nor should she. Martha's work is significant, but her significance is no longer in her work.

MARTHA'S FAITH JOURNEY: FROM FRUSTRATION TO FAITH

Martha may have a few faults, but her journey is far from over. She learns from her mistakes, and she keeps serving. She doesn't force Mary into the kitchen and she doesn't dismiss Jesus' advice or question his authority. Instead, she continues to follow. She continues to believe. And the best is yet to come.

During the last weeks of Jesus' life, he has an unprecedented encounter with Martha. Her brother Lazarus is deathly ill. Martha knows that Jesus alone can make the situation right. She has him on speed dial. So she calls him and asks him to come. Immediately.

But he doesn't come right away. Imagine her disappointment. She waits and waits over three days. Her brother dies. Why didn't Jesus doesn't respond sooner? She is both crushed and confused. When Jesus finally arrives on the scene—albeit too late—she still runs to meet him. She still takes the initiative.

> "Lord," Martha said to Jesus, "if you had been
> here, my brother would not have died. But I know

that even now God will give you whatever you ask."[13]

Jesus quickly comforts Martha and tells her, "Your brother will rise again."[14] But he also asks her to proclaim her faith.

> Jesus said to her, "I am the resurrection and the life. The one who believes in me will live, even though they die; and whoever lives by believing in me will never die. Do you believe this?"[15]

Martha doesn't hesitate. Her faith is based on who Jesus is—not what she is doing for him.

> "Yes Lord" she told him, "I believe that you are the Christ, the Son of God, who was to come into the world."[16]

There are no strings attached. No performance exams to take. Martha's faith is secure. And while she needs Jesus desperately, she doesn't make any demands. She doesn't stomp her feet and proclaim that life is unfair. She doesn't scold Jesus for arriving too late or blame Mary for the situation. But she does leave the door open for Jesus to act.

"But I know that even now God will give you whatever you ask."[17]

She believes, but her belief is not conditional on Jesus' performance. It is based on who he is. She places her burdens at Jesus' feet.

In Jesus' last miracle before his own death, he raises Lazarus from the dead. His work on earth is almost done, and he saves his greatest work short of Calvary—raising a man who had been dead for four days—for none other than Martha! Yet this miracle is not a condition of Martha's faith. He doesn't act to make her believe; he acts because she believes. Martha has already given Jesus her heart.

I love this about Jesus. He is patient with us on each of our journeys. He waits until we are ready, and then he wows us with the unexpected. When Martha invites Jesus into her home for a dinner party, she never expects that he will change her life. She may have seen Jesus as a wise religious teacher, but he gives her so much more.

Like Martha, we may think we just signed up for a casual religious experience, but Jesus has something better in mind. He wants to give us more. He takes great delight in lavishing miracles on women who are tired, stressed, and overworked. Like Martha, he longs to change our life and work forever.

BEING A MODERN-DAY MARTHA

Too often, we leave Martha in the kitchen, stomping her feet and blaming her sister. We don't give her credit where credit is due. Martha aches for every woman who is carrying too much, working too hard, and juggling too many roles. Martha gets it. She gets us. She knows what it's like to wake up on Easter morning and instead of focusing on what's important—a risen Lord—she's fussing over all the details.

Martha knows what it's like to learn the hard way. But she doesn't let her mistakes bring her down, and she's not too stubborn to change. She swallows her pride. She keeps working. She proclaims her faith. And, in the process, she doesn't run from the work God puts before her. With Jesus' help, Martha becomes the woman God created.

Discussion Questions for Chapter Eleven

1. Contrast Martha and Mary. Why is it so hard for Martha to sit at Jesus' feet? Why does it come so naturally for Mary?

2. Can you relate to the "Martha Syndrome"? With which symptom do you most identify?

3. Read Matthew 11:28–29. What are some of the heavy burdens you carry?

4. Notice how Martha's faith grows and changes. What do you appreciate most about her story?

ə• *Select readings:* Luke chapter 10; John chapter 11

CHAPTER ELEVEN NOTES

1. Luke 10: 38–42.
2. Luke 10:38.
3. Luke 10:40.
4. Luke 10:41–42a.
5. Luke 10:42b.
6. Luke 7:37–38.
7. Luke 7:47.
8. John 11:2.
9. Most scholars point to the fact that the Luke 7 account is in the home of Simon the Pharisee, a considerable distance from Bethany, and took place during Jesus' ministry in Galilee. The John 12 account (where Mary of Bethany is clearly referenced) is in the home of Simon the leper, immediately preceding Jesus' death. I tend to think they are different events (with perhaps different women), but I leave open the possibility that Mary of Bethany could have anointed Jesus in Luke 7. In any event, she displays the humility of a forgiven sinner.
10. Ephesians 2:8–9.
11. Matt 11:28–29.
12. John 12:2.
13. John 11:21–22.
14. John 11: 23.
15. John 11:25.
16. John 11:27.
17. John 11:22.

Chapter Twelve

LYDIA

Finding Your Own Style

Some women are born with their own style. Lydia of Philippi is such a woman.

Lydia stands in a class of her own. She is *both* cool and spiritual. And she doesn't apologize for either.

To start, Lydia is wildly successful in business. She undoubtedly represents the "new" modern woman of her day—a businesswoman who enjoys profitable trading throughout the Greco-Roman world. Lydia is a dealer in purple cloth—at a time when purple dye is the most expensive and sought-after dye in the Roman world. Which means Lydia has plenty of capital. As a seller of purple, expensive, and even royal textiles, she is probably one of the richest and most influential women in her region.

I like to imagine Lydia as not just selling purple, but wearing it. And not just wearing it, but wearing it well. Lydia is the type of woman that you meet at a party and gawk, *Where did you ever get that outfit?* She's the kind of woman that we all want to emulate. She sets the trends. And she's not afraid to be the woman God created.

Who knows, maybe Lydia even authored the phrase, *When you've got it, flaunt it!*

MY OWN LYDIA

I have a special place in my heart for Lydia. Maybe it's because I live with her.

My middle daughter, Anna, has her own style. Let's just say she makes her own fashion choices, with little input from Mom.

When Anna was in kindergarten, my husband was picking her up at school when one of the teachers—a teacher we had never met before—stopped him.

"Hey, we were all talking about Anna the other day—the way she dresses. Anyway, we all decided that her mother must have been a big hippie or something."

He just laughed and said, "Her mother is a lawyer. She isn't exactly the hippie type."

I had a good laugh as well. Anna went through a phase when she would only wear her headbands "bandana style"—the Cheech and Chong look, but on a first grader. In the midst of my distress, a good friend reassured me that Anna is on the cutting edge of fashion. Hollywood has apparently embraced bandana style. It just hasn't hit the mainstream yet.

I could stress out over it. I can just hear the neighbors talking behind my back. *What kind of mother would let her daughter dress like a hippie?*

Instead, I am comforted by the fact that Anna is just like Lydia. Lydia's style didn't seem to slow her down. If anything, it probably enhanced her business. Who says women can't be fashion queens *and* love Jesus? As we'll see, Lydia's outward appearance is only a small part of her legacy. Lydia isn't just a fashion queen and powerful businesswoman; she's one of the most influential leaders in the early Christian church.

A Woman in Demand

Lydia is mentioned by name only twice in the Bible—both times in Acts 16. But we can learn much about her through context and history. To start, Lydia is likely Greek. While she is living and working in the city of Philippi, her hometown is Thyatira— part of the old kingdom of Lydia, where she undoubtedly gets her name.

Thyatira is located in Asia Minor, part of western Turkey. It is famous for valuable trading, including indigo and dyes. In addition to Thyatira, the province of Lydia includes four additional cities (Ephesus, Smyrna, Sardis, and Philadelphia) on or near major rivers, which make the region a natural center of commerce.

In Lydia's region, cloth could be dyed purple by several methods. The most costly and famous method was the Tyrian purple of Rome, reserved for royalty and made from a rare saltwater snail. The more common method involved combining two plants—indigo (dark blue) and rose madder (red). This inferior purple dye, worn by the common people, was fermented in urine and often produced near rivers, perhaps part of the reason Lydia is hanging out at a riverbank outside of town.[1] Regardless of whether Lydia deals in royal or common dye, one thing is certain. Purple is in demand in the Roman world. Which means Lydia is likewise in demand.

In addition to being a busy businesswoman, Lydia manages a household. No husband is mentioned, and the composition of her home is largely unknown. She may be a widow, single mom, or caregiver of extended family. The fact that Lydia is named after a region causes some historians to believe her roots are in slavery. But, regardless of her origins, Lydia is a free woman when we meet her in Philippi. She is independent in business, a homeowner, and the likely head of her home. She knows what it's like to be the breadwinner, and she is comfortable being in charge.

GOD FIRST, BUSINESS SECOND

This brings me to what I love most about Lydia. She's got moxie. But not just moxie for the sake of moxie. Moxie for Jesus.

According to the Apostle Paul, he bumps into Lydia on the Sabbath. Lydia isn't a Jew, but she also hasn't bought into the pagan gods of her culture. Instead, she worships the God of Israel. When she first meets Paul, she is gathering with a group of other women on the shores of the river Gangites. Acts 16 describes this first encounter:

> On the Sabbath we went outside the city gate to the river, where we expected to find a place of prayer. We sat down and began to speak to the women who had gathered there. One of those listening was a woman from the city of Thyatira named Lydia, a dealer in purple cloth. She was

a worshiper of God. The Lord opened her heart to respond to Paul's message. When she and the members of her household were baptized, she invited us to her home. "If you consider me a believer in the Lord," she said, "come and stay at my house." And she persuaded us.[2]

Lydia is sometimes called the first European convert to Christianity. Her conversion is remarkable in several respects.

First, she is extremely decisive. She doesn't tell Paul, *Come back in a week and I'll let you know what I decide about Jesus.* She doesn't worry about how her newfound faith will impact her business. She just believes. Wholeheartedly.

In Lydia's day, she embraces a brand-new faith—a faith her customers of purple dye don't share. If she is the first convert, none of her customers are Christians. Some of them might even laugh at her and cancel their business contracts. Others probably purchase purple cloth for pagan temple curtains and for costumes of pagan idols. Still other customers are perhaps part of the imperial Roman family.[3] What would they think of Lydia once she became a Christian?

Yet Lydia isn't paralyzed about fears of what people will think. This doesn't mean she doesn't count the cost. She just decides it is worth it.

A New Purpose in Work

Given Lydia's conversion, she may have doubted her ability to continue as a profitable trader. How could she stay committed to her home and business while playing a leadership role in a growing church? How could she juggle the priorities and demands of apparently competing worlds? Surely, doubts crossed her mind as she wrestled with seemingly conflicting roles.

I think I'm going to have to give up purple dye forever. Sure, I know I have expensive taste, but from now on I'm going to have to shop at the local resale shop and stay away from bright colors. After all, I don't want to draw attention to myself. I need to change my priorities and get out of the rat race.

We don't know the details of Lydia's business before or after she meets Paul. But every indication is that Lydia keeps working. Sure, she had a radical conversion. But that doesn't mean she gives up her business. It doesn't mean she stops being a fashion queen.

How else could she keep her home, provide shelter for the apostles, and provide a meeting place for the church? Once Lydia and her household are baptized, she invites Paul and his colleagues into her home. And she doesn't just invite them, she *persuades* them.

> "If you consider me a believer in the Lord," she said, "come and stay at my house." And she persuaded us.[4]

Lydia is immediately willing (even anxious) to give of her resources. She doesn't want to sit back and enjoy her profits while the apostles sleep on the streets. She wants to make an impact. And she doesn't just want her home to be a place of shelter. It becomes a place of refuge and gathering for the early Christians in Philippi.

Hosting Church in Style

By opening her home to the church, Lydia merges her worlds. By working in the center of commerce, Lydia continues to be culturally relevant. Which makes her well positioned to minister to the world around her. Her peers see that followers of Christ aren't all that weird. After all, if someone like Lydia has found truth and meaning, Christians may be on to something.

Lydia changes her priorities. She realigns her resources. But I don't believe she changes her style.

We have much to gain from Lydia's style. Many of us expect Christian women to be culturally insulated—even dull and boring. We've bought into a lie that we lack spiritual depth if we like to shop or wear leopard-skin pants or paint our toenails bright red. Even worse, some career women think they have to give up their style first in order to follow Christ. I once heard a pastor refer to this myth as the "second conversion." Once new Christians come to faith, they think they have to conform to a set of "Christian" cultural norms. They have to dress a certain way, attend certain church functions, and abstain from certain activities. It's all rather exhausting.

I'm not buying it. And neither is Lydia. This high-powered dealer in purple cloth may have risked her career for her faith. But she did so being a first-century power woman. Not a shrinking violent.

Besides, I'm convinced Lydia liked to shop.

Overcoming the Fashion Police

You don't have to confine yourself to Christian circles to run into the fashion police. Everyone is trying to tell women how to dress. Including other women.

I was at a businesswomen's conference, and the organizers decided to bring in a fashion consultant. In hindsight, I think it was for comic relief. The consultant was downright condescending and, in my opinion, plain wrong.

"Don't wear Ann Taylor or St. John. It makes you look like you're wearing a uniform. Don't wear bright colors and patterns. It makes you seem indecisive. If you're thin, don't wear your skirts too long. If you're fat, don't wear your skirts too short. Wear dark colors in business, and invest in a couple of neutral tailored jackets."

In other words, dress like a man.

I just remember thinking to myself, *I'm so tired of everyone telling women how to dress. Here I am at a professional women's conference. Most of us are struggling with the demands of work, home, and business and we can't find something better to talk about?*

Apparently not. While I'm all for being professional, there is something that sucks the life right out of us when we have to conform for the sake of conforming. The women at the conference were so outraged that they started booing the consultant—a sight in and of itself. The audience included my friends Monique and Deb, both hard-core trial lawyers. They also aren't very good at conforming.

To start, we had a good laugh over the comments about "dark" suits. Deb—the most seasoned trial lawyer you will ever meet—explained that she and her female colleagues coordinate their outfits during jury trials. They trade off wearing fuchsia.

The men on the other side are always wearing black and grey. And, yes, the women tend to stand out. They tend to win cases in style!

Like Deb and Monique, Lydia probably wore fuchsia with regularity. She's bold about her style. And she's likewise bold about her faith. When the rubber hits the road, Lydia isn't afraid to risk everything.

Lydia Risks Everything

Lydia is so much more than a fashion queen. As if her conversion isn't bold enough, Lydia next decides to risk her life for her new faith. Paul and his companion Silas are flogged, beaten, and thrown into prison soon after they arrive in Philippi. This would have been the perfect time for Lydia to get out. Or at least go under cover and be a closet Christian. Is following Jesus worth this much trouble? It's one thing to be affiliated with a minority religion. It's another thing to join forces with common criminals.

Pleasing the local government isn't a high priority for Paul. In fact, he has a way of causing trouble wherever he goes. In Philippi, he rescues a demented slave girl and heals her from infirmity. Her master, who has exploited the girl for years, complains that Paul and Silas have ruined his business. He lodges a formal complaint against Paul and Silas, and they are dragged into the marketplace where they are publically humiliated before being thrown into prison.

Paul doesn't know how to fly under the radar. He doesn't even try. Being a Christian means upsetting the status quo. What has Lydia gotten herself into? Yet she doesn't run the other way. She doesn't tell Paul to keep his distance. Just the opposite. When Paul and Silas are released from prison, guess where they head? Straight to Lydia's house. That's right, she risks her own neck (and probably the safety of her family) to give them a shelter and haven. Lydia's door remains wide open. In fact, Lydia's home isn't just a haven—it becomes the official meeting place for the first church in Philippi.

How's that for a little business development!

LYDIA'S LEGACY—THE PHILIPPIAN CHURCH

Although Lydia isn't mentioned by name after Acts 16, we follow her legacy through the church of Philippi. In his letter to the Philippians, Paul lavishes praise and thanksgiving on the church:

> I thank my God every time I remember you. In all my prayers for all of you, I always pray with joy because of your partnership in the gospel *from the first day until now*, being confident of this, that he who began a good work in you will carry it on to completion until the day of Christ Jesus.[5]

Paul is likely referring to that *first day* on the river Gangites when he met Lydia. We know that Lydia is the first convert in Philippi. She is among the first to be baptized and the first to open her home. In many ways, Lydia is the mother of the Philippians—a church populated with strong women. If Paul hesitated to leave Philippi in the hands of a group of women, he certainly doesn't show it in his writings. He goes on to write to the Philippians that "I have you in my heart" (v. 7) and "I long for all of you with the affection of Christ Jesus" (v. 8). This church is his "joy and crown" (4:1).

In a predominately male culture, Paul addresses the women in the church as partners. The Philippian church is far from perfect, but it appears healthy and functional. For example, in urging two women in Philippi to settle a dispute for the sake of unity, Paul doesn't scold or belittle them. Instead, he addresses them by name as "women who have contended at my side in the cause of the gospel."[6] No doubt these women have lived and learned from Lydia.

Lydia's Generosity Is Contagious

The Philippian church is likewise a model for stewardship. Paul commends this generosity repeatedly,

- "When I set out from Macedonia, not one church shared with me in the matter of giving and receiving, *except you only.*"[7]
- "Even when I was in Thessalonica, you sent me aid again and again when I was in need."[8]
- "I am amply supplied, now that I have received from Epaphroditus the gifts you sent."[9]

Even in infancy, the Philippian church sees a need, steps up, and gives. They don't send Paul off empty-handed; they send him aid on the road, and they even bring him gifts in prison. No one told them to give. No other church modeled giving. So how did this infant church become so generous?

Lydia's influence undoubtedly prevailed. Many believe that Lydia's wealth provides for Paul on his many journeys.[10] Lydia uses her style and resources—her two greatest assets—for something bigger and better than trading purple dye. She doesn't apologize for the platform God has given her; she leverages her platform. And, in the process, God shows us what a Greco-Roman purple powerhouse can do for Jesus.

How's that for a legacy?

CHANGING OUR HEARTS, NOT OUR STYLE

Not many of us deal in purple dye for a living. Maybe we're not high on fashion or we don't know how to accessorize. No one gawks at us at parties (at least not to compliment us!) and we don't set the trends. But we each have our own style.

Likewise, not many of us have risked our careers for our faith. We haven't harbored fugitives who are running from the authorities or sent aid to our friends in prison. We continue to go about our work and play it safe. But we each have our own resources.

Like Lydia, God longs to use our unique style and resources for a greater good. It's never easy to follow Jesus in style. Frankly, it would be easier to follow some cookie-cutter formula or one-size-fits-all method to spiritual living. An authentic faith is much more complex. It was hard for Lydia, and it's just as hard for us. How do I share the love of Jesus with a client who doesn't share my faith? How can I be culturally relevant when my culture doesn't share my values? How do I give of my time and resources when I am already stretched so thin?

Too many women around us are trying to fake it. Some of us are even faking it because we think we have to—that we won't be accepted by God if we keep our style. Lydia shows us that we don't have to shed our passions to follow Jesus. While she doesn't have easy answers, she shows us that God is in the business of changing our hearts, not our style.

What's Lydia's secret? *Change your heart. Give your resources. Keep your style.*

Which is why I will never prohibit Anna from wearing hippie clothes.

Discussion Questions for Chapter Twelve

1. Can you think of a modern-day Lydia? What does Lydia teach us about being successful in faith and business?

2. Consider Lydia's conversion and decision to host the New Testament church in her home. What is she risking?

3. Lydia's legacy lives through the church of Philippi. Consider your own legacy. What kind of mark will you leave behind?

ᐓ *Select readings:* Acts chapter 16

CHAPTER TWELVE NOTES

1. "Women of the Bible: Lydia," *Daily Devotion Blog*, http://dailyprayer.us/daily_devotion_blog/?p=29.
2. Acts 16:13–15.
3. Deen, *All the Women of the Bible*, 224–25.
4. Acts 16:15.
5. Philippians 1:3–6 (emphasis added).
6. Philippians 4:3.
7. Philippians 4:15 (emphasis added).
8. Philippians 4:16.
9. Philippians 4:18.
10. James, *Lost Women of the Bible*, 216–17.

PRISCILLA
God's Design for Equal Work

Where are the men in this book? As we study the working women of the Bible, we notice that many of them are single or widowed. Even if they are married, there is little mention of men playing a prominent role in their lives. Sure, women like Rahab and Esther knew how to work a male-dominated society to their advantage, but we can argue that men are part of the problem in such instances, exploiting these women based on social status and gender. If we're not careful, we might conclude that working women in the Bible don't need men at all.

But that's not the point. This study isn't intended to blame men or ignore their contributions. As we wrestle with the lives and lessons of the women of the Bible, we see that women and men have struggled to live and work together throughout history. The Bible records this tension, consistent with other historical sources.

I know what you're thinking. I'm thinking the same thing. *Is it even possible for men and women to work together in harmony?*

Is work so twisted and broken in this world that it's not even worth the effort?

Thankfully, we have Priscilla as a role model. She shows us that it's not just possible—it's profitable. And we can't study Priscilla in isolation; we likewise need to meet her husband, Aquila. Together, Priscilla and Aquila are a New Testament model for teamwork, equality, and harmony in both work and marriage.

INTERDEPENDENT, NOT CODEPENDENT

God created women and men to be partners—interdependent and equal partners. Regardless of whether we are single or married, God wants the men in our lives to complement our work, not threaten it. Which is why I'm so thankful for Priscilla and Aquila. God knows we need their example—not only for the first century church but for *our* generation.

Priscilla and Aquila may be the least-talked-about power couple in the Bible. They aren't bold or flashy. They don't engage in or seek out drama. They work. They travel. They lead the church. They don't ask for praise or recognition.

The first thing I notice about them is that they are always together. She doesn't go anywhere without him. He doesn't go anywhere without her. They are like two peas in a pod. Priscilla and Aquila. Aquila and Priscilla.

In fact, of the seven times they are mentioned by name in the Bible, they are always mentioned together.[1] They seem to take the phrase *till death do us part* both figuratively and literally—they are completely joined at the hip!

Does this mean they are weak? That they don't have their own identities? In our society today, we'd probably make fun of them. We'd probably see Priscilla as lacking confidence and independence. *What's the matter with her? She needs to get her own life. She needs to stand on her own.* We'd probably likewise criticize Aquila as lacking backbone or leadership. *What kind of guy hangs out with his wife all the time? He's such a weakling. I wonder if he even goes to the bathroom without her.*

Yet when we set aside our modern prejudices, we see a team that is interdependent—not codependent or dysfunctional. And their interdependence is a model for good work.

Priscilla and Aquila thrive off one another—both vocationally and spiritually. They strengthen each other; they don't pull each other down. How many married couples can work together every day without driving each other crazy? These two don't just work together. They *like* working together. And they do it well.

Partners in Business and in Faith

When Paul meets Priscilla and Aquila, they are in Corinth working side by side. Yet they aren't a closed team of two. They welcome Paul into their business.

> Paul left Athens and went to Corinth. There he met a Jew named Aquila, a native of Pontus, who had recently come from Italy with his wife Priscilla, because Claudius had ordered all the Jews to leave Rome. Paul went to see them, and because he was a tentmaker as they were, he stayed and worked with them.[2]

Isn't it admirable that Priscilla and Aquila share their trade with the Apostle Paul—a complete stranger? They take him into their business and likely into their home. Paul affirms that their work is important. Paul doesn't complain about having to be a tentmaker or demean their work as secular or commercial. He doesn't say, *Rats! I have to go make tents to earn some money before I can get on to more important things.* Instead, he *stays* with them and *works.* He recognizes the value of earning a living.

Working side by side with Priscilla and Aquila, Paul develops a deep friendship and lasting bond. Together, they will impact and grow the early church in multiple cities.

And it all starts with making tents together.

Paul shows us not to underestimate relationships with our co-workers. When we work side by side with others, we really get to know them. We learn about their habits, their values, and their character. We see their strengths and weaknesses, and we learn what makes them thrive.

In this case, Paul quickly sees Priscilla and Aquila as a unit. They are a package deal. And the three of them together—Paul, Priscilla, and Aquila—form a chord not easily broken. Priscilla and Aquila aren't the kind of couple that makes a single guy like Paul feel like a third wheel. To the contrary, their interdependence is an asset in welcoming Paul into the team. They become partners not just in business but in faith.

> "For where two or three gather together as my followers, I am there among them."[3]

PARTNERS IN EXILE

It's likewise important to understand how Priscilla and Aquila end up in Corinth. They aren't just partners; they are partners in exile. They have just been expelled from Rome, likely over a public dispute between Jews and Christians. We can assume that Aquila is Jewish by birth. Priscilla may also be Jewish, or perhaps she is of Mediterranean origin. Regardless of her heritage, one thing is certain. When the Jews are expelled from Rome, they both leave. She doesn't say, "See you in a few years. I'll stay in Rome and let you know when it's safe to return." No, she's committed to join her husband in exile. For better or for worse, they are in this together.

They likely travel to Corinth by sea (a journey of more than six hundred miles). When they arrive, business is booming. Corinth is an entrepreneurial choice to set up shop. It hosts two ports—both strategic stops for Mediterranean goods headed to Europe.[4] And it's also a place of cultural, moral, and ethnic diversity. For a couple used to being in Rome, it's a chance to start over—both personally and professionally.

We don't know if Pricilla and Aquila have children who travel with them. The text is silent, but I think it's likely they are caregivers, perhaps to extended family. If they have children, it's possible they accompany their parents in the marketplace and work alongside them. After all, it's a family business.

There's no indication that Aquila leads the family business. There's also no indication that Priscilla leads the family business. They work together, as partners in love *and* business. Neither is tied to a particular role, although they likely divide the tasks. They play to each other's strengths and work as a team. Priscilla may have managed the finances and marketing plan while Aquila managed the workers and inventory. Since tents in those days were made of both leather and goat hair, they may also work as leatherworkers or saddlers.[5] Regardless of the specifics of their trade, they are clearly in a thriving partnership.

Some have argued that Priscilla was the "leader" of this relationship since her name is usually mentioned first when the couple is referenced[6]—an unusual practice in a male-dominated society. She may have been the more prominent of the two or carried greater weight with the New Testament audience. That being said, Aquila is mentioned first in several references.[7] Which again confirms they are a unit—it's not about being first or second.

A TEAM ON THE MOVE

Priscilla and Aquila don't get complacent. They don't have the luxury. Once they get their business up and running in Corinth, it's time to make another move. They have already been thrown out of Rome, and it feels like they are just settling in. But there's no time to sit back and relax. There's no time to get cozy and comfortable. Being comfortable isn't the goal. They're part of a movement that is changing history.

It's an exciting and scary time to be in business with Paul. As they work together in Corinth for over eighteen months, Paul persuades both Jews and Greeks that Jesus is the Christ. But he stirs up some controversy in the process. Some of the Jews oppose him, and he moves his preaching from the synagogue to the house of Justus. Even the synagogue ruler and his family come to believe. Many are baptized. But others are outraged. As in Philippi, Paul tends to upset the status quo wherever he goes. Corinth is no exception. Paul's preaching in the synagogue isn't welcomed by all, and he is tried in the local courts for heresy.

Priscilla and Aquila are tightly aligned with Paul. Such ties prove costly—both personally and professionally. It's time for Paul to get out of town. Which means it's also time for Priscilla and Aquila to get out of town. We don't know whether they are forced to leave or whether they leave by choice. We do know that they all leave together—Paul, Priscilla, and Aquila. They set out for Syria and on to Ephesus. Mind you, they've barely had time to get settled in Corinth. Starting over with nothing is never good for business. But Priscilla and Aquila have caught the vision. They are in deep, and there is no turning back. If Jesus is real, he is worth everything. Since Paul is on the move, they decide to move with him. They count the cost together. It's worth the risk.

So they leave everything behind and move again.

I wonder if it bothered Priscilla that she didn't have a home of her own. Living out of a suitcase probably isn't what she planned when she married Aquila. Surely she hoped for some stability. A nest egg. A place to plant a garden and invite her friends over for tea. But Priscilla isn't caught up in keeping up with the neighbors. She probably doesn't fit in with the local "wives club." The women in town may think she is overbearing and intimidating. Or that she doesn't have her priorities in order. Why spend all that time at the market running a business? Why risk everything for her newfound faith? Doesn't she want a stable home?

Priscilla knows that *home* is a relative term. Home isn't about bricks and mortar. It's not dependent on the perfect décor or the latest trends. It's not even about stability or security. It's a matter of the heart. Besides, she knows that the suburbs can get boring and predictable. It's much more fun to follow Jesus in reckless abandon. And she couldn't have a better partner than Aquila to share the journey.

HOMELESS AND JOBLESS?

We can learn a few things from Priscilla's outlook on life. While making a home is a worthy endeavor, too many women are completely obsessed with the outward structure of our lives. We're unsettled when we have to "move" our homes—and I'm not just talking about a physical move. The slightest change in our location, vocation, or comfort zone has a way of upsetting the applecart and freaking us out.

I can't imagine relocating to a new city at this stage of life. Nor can I imagine leaving everything—my work, my home, my security blankets. My kids are settled into their schools and social networks. I've worked hard to build my professional ties and reputation. Nothing about starting over sounds appealing. The last thing I want to do is be homeless and jobless. Dare I say I'm not even open to radical change?

Not so with Priscilla. I admire her perspective and adventurous spirit. I also admire her guts and pure zeal. By aligning her family with a political and social outcast like Paul, she prepares to give up everything. The little house with the white picket fence is out of the question. She knows her reward will be eternal—and that the gain will be exponential. Sure, it may be inconvenient in the process. But, together with her husband, she has the chance to make history. So she doesn't look back. She leaves Corinth and sails again for uncharted waters.

If Paul has other companions on the journey to Ephesus, they are unnamed. So far as we know, it's the dynamic threesome—Paul,

Priscilla, and Aquila. After arriving in Ephesus, Paul leaves Pricilla and Aquila behind and then heads to Jerusalem. Priscilla and Aquila ask him to stay, but he declines. So Priscilla and Aquila are left in Ephesus without Paul. Rather than pouting or heading back to Corinth, they get to work.

Priscilla and Aquila go on to establish the church in Ephesus. They teach, host, and lead—by example and by instruction. They meet Apollo, a talented young preacher, and together confront him when he delivers an incomplete message. They don't embarrass or scold him; they quietly pull him aside and correct him. Together.[8]

The church in Ephesus starts meeting in their home. They again risk social and political persecution. And the church in Ephesus thrives. With their nourishment and support, a young disciple named Timothy becomes a faithful leader.

We're not sure if Priscilla and Aquila continue their business in Ephesus. They may have continued their trade as tentmakers—to pay the bills and help support the church. But it's likewise possible that they devoted their full efforts to the work of the church. After all, they host the local church, provide instruction in teaching, and nurture the local body. They more than make their mark in Ephesus.

Yet Priscilla and Aquila don't stay in Ephesus. Things are about to come full circle.

RIGHT BACK WHERE THEY STARTED

Priscilla probably never expected to return to her old stomping grounds. When she left her life in Rome behind, she likely said good-bye forever. But sometimes, God brings us right back where we started. After the Emperor Claudius dies, it is safe for Jews to return to Rome. Aquila and Priscilla decide to make the journey.

When they return to Rome, they are changed. Their travels have made them stronger and wiser. Their faith is deeper and wider. They have witnessed miracles, experienced persecution, and built friendships that will last forever. They may have been followers of Jesus when they started their travels, but now they are disciples. They are leaders in the church.

And their work is far from over.

Paul's greeting to them in Rome applauds their work:

> Greet Priscilla and Aquila my helpers in Christ Jesus:
> Who have for my life laid down their own necks: unto whom not only I give thanks, but also all the churches of the Gentiles.
> Likewise greet the church that is in their house.[9]

We learn so much from this greeting. We see that the adventure has paid off—and it continues. Paul refers to them as helpers, not servants. This word *helper* applies equally to Priscilla—she is even referenced first. Her contribution isn't limited by her gender. Paul uses the same Greek word to describe his relationship with men in leadership throughout the church, including Timothy and Titus.[10]

Priscilla and Aquila have "laid down their necks" for Paul. What better friends could he have? All the Gentile churches are thankful for their service.

Finally, we see that even in Rome they are again hosting the church in their home. Maybe it doesn't have a white picket fence, but its door is wide open.

Before we conclude they lived happily ever after in Rome, think again. Change is the name of the game, and this duo will again move back to Ephesus. In Paul's final letter to Timothy (well after Paul's letter to the Romans), he greets "Priscilla and Aquila" one last time—back in Ephesus![11]

They are again on the move. Probably to finish the work they started with the Ephesian church. I doubt they enjoyed an uneventful and relaxing retirement. Instead they enjoyed a life of partnership and purpose. There is still work to be done, and they aren't about to slow down—they're just not cut out for retirement.

A MODEL IN LIFE AND LOVE

Priscilla and Aquila set the bar. And they set it high. We can't help but contrast their relationship with most marriages in biblical history—and most marriages today. They clearly stand apart as equal contributors. No, I'm not suggesting they're perfect. I'm sure they had their disappointments and annoyances, just like the rest of us. But they model a partnership worth emulating. A partnership based on gifting and strengths—not roles and stereotypes.

It's not like Priscilla and Aquila are on the fringes of the New Testament church. They are in the center. They are part of the core leadership. They are in Paul's inner circle. He repeatedly calls them out as his most trusted and valued friends. They have a partnership that is not only admirable, it is divine.

Priscilla and Aquila's actions speak louder than words. They answer the question that is burning in our hearts and minds.

How do women and men live and work together in harmony?

The answer is simple yet complicated. History disappoints us, yet we've come a long way from the garden of Eden. There is bad news and good news. The bad news is that it's really hard—some would say impossible—for men and women to thrive in harmony. But the good news far outweighs the bad. The good news is that it depends on God, not us.

> "Humanly speaking, it is impossible. But with God everything is possible."[12]

Discussion Questions for Chapter Thirteen

1. What are some of the traits that make Priscilla and Aquila a successful team? How do they break the stereotypes of men and women working together in business?

2. Imagine constantly relocating your home and business. How do you think Priscilla dealt with this type of lifestyle?

3. What is it about work that enables us to really bond? Notice how Priscilla and Aquila bond with Paul as they work together. Have you ever experienced this type of relationship with your co-workers?

ఎ *Select readings:* Acts chapter 16

CHAPTER THIRTEEN NOTES

1.   See Acts 18:2, 18, 26; Romans 16:3; 1 Corinthians 16:19; and 2 Timothy 4:19. In the seventh mention of this couple (Acts 18:19–21) they are referred to as a unit, emphasizing their combined role.

2.   Acts 18: 1b–3.

3.   Matt 18:20 (NLT).

4.   Owens, *Daughters of Eve*, 212–13.

5.   Ibid., 212.

6.   Acts 18:18, 26; Romans 16:3; 2 Timothy 4:19.

7.   Acts 18:2; 1 Corinthians 16:19.

8.   Acts 18:26.

9.   Romans 16:3-5a (KJV).

10. Romans 16:21; 2 Corinthians 8:23.

11. 2 Timothy 4:19.

12. Matthew 19:26 (NLT).

Chapter Fourteen

JESUS

The Timeless Mentor

The working women of the Bible are some of the most remarkable women we will ever meet. We celebrate their successes and learn from their failures. We long for their strength and determination. Their stories are our stories. Their joy is our joy. Their pain is our pain.

Yet, for all of their triumphs, each of them is human. Just like us. And, beginning with Eve, their work is broken. At the prime of her life, Ruth is alone and homeless. Esther may be a beauty queen, but she hides her true identity to climb to the top. Martha has resources, but she is stressed out and overworked. Some things have gone right, but many things have gone wrong.

There is no easy road. Not for them. Not for us. Author and business executive Diane Paddison puts it bluntly: "Men *pretend* everything's fine, while women just work harder and harder to try and make everything fine."[1]

Is this really what God intended? That we struggle this hard in our work?

If we stop here, the best we can do is try harder. Work harder. Work smarter.

But some of us can't work any harder. And this is old news. We long to hear something different.

This is where Jesus enters the picture. I have been a follower of Christ for more than thirty years. Sure, I've had my doubts and struggles, but I keep following him for a simple reason:

He offers something different.

In a noisy and confused world, Jesus sees that our work is twisted and broken. So he steps in to change our plight. He doesn't just *tell* us what to do. He *shows* us what to do.

Jesus *models* work, *values* work, and *transforms* work. And he gets it done through the incredible. He takes on human form and submits himself to earthly work.

JESUS THE WORKER BEE: MODELING WORK

To start, Jesus knows what it's like to work. I mean *really* work. While many of us envision Jesus sitting next to the throne of God, we miss the fact that he is a worker bee—like you and me—for the first thirty years of his life on earth.

Jesus works as a middle-class carpenter. He builds things. He knows what it's like to get his hands dirty. He gets blisters. He pounds nails. He has to meet deadlines. He knows what it's like to deal with an unreasonable customer or an unreliable supplier. There is no one more emphatic to our earthly toil than Jesus.

I missed this for years—the fact that Jesus had a regular job before his public ministry—until I read *Work Matters* by Tom Nelson. As Nelson explains:

> Here was the Son of God sent to earth on a
> redemptive mission of seeking and saving the
> lost, of proclaiming the gospel, yet he spent the
> vast majority of his years on earth making things
> in an obscure carpentry shop. . . . At first glance
> it doesn't seem to be a very strategic use of the
> Son of God's extraordinary gifts or his important
> messianic mission.[2]

If Jesus was trying to build his resume, he could have done better. It must have been frustrating to work within the confines of the human body making furniture for people's houses. Making a wooden bench just doesn't compare to setting the stars and moon in place. It's more than a demotion for the creator of the universe!

To make matters worse, Jesus' background as a carpenter arguably makes him less credible when he starts his public ministry. He is too "common"—especially in his hometown—to command any authority. The people don't just ignore him, they mock him:

> "Isn't this *the carpenter*? Isn't this Mary's son and
> the brother of James, Joseph, Judas and Simon?
> Aren't his sisters here with us?" And they took
> offense at him.[3]

I don't know why Jesus chose carpentry over a position of religious or political importance. Maybe it's God's sheer love of irony. Maybe it's to teach us not to rely on human power or status. Or maybe it's to simply allow Jesus to better empathize with our work.

Jesus knows what it's like to be overqualified and undervalued. Yet he still submits to his earthly work as a carpenter. It's the most surprising example of patience and humility in daily work we can fathom. At the ripe age of thirty, Jesus, the Son of God, appears stuck in a dead-end career with no upward mobility. Surely, he feels frustrated as he waits. Has God forgotten completely about his resume?

When we see Jesus' humility and faithfulness as a carpenter, something about our daily work doesn't seem so bad. If the Son of God can pound nails for a living, an honest day's work isn't beneath us either. Besides, God isn't likely done with us. If Jesus can work as he waits, so can we.

JESUS THE BUSINESS CONSULTANT: VALUING WORK

Jesus not only models work, he values work. I never pictured Jesus as a business consultant until I read *At Work as It Is in Heaven* by J. B. Wood. Wood describes Jesus' "brief stint as a management consultant"[4] based on the account in John, chapter 21. After Jesus rises from the dead, Peter and a few other disciples go out fishing. In other words, they go back to their old jobs. Who can blame them? After all, they have to earn a living.

They are out all night trying to catch fish, and they come up empty-handed. Jesus appears on the shore the next morning. Like any good consultant, he suggests the obvious—put your nets of the other side of the boat. The disciples oblige, and the fish are so plentiful that the boat overflows!

Why does he perform this miracle? It certainly isn't to convince them he is the Son of God—he has already returned from the dead. Some would say he is now teaching them a lesson about their pending career change—a soft kick to get them out of the boat and onto the shore. Maybe so, but in the process, he also blesses them with a ton of fish. In doing so, he values their work. He could have called them to shore and said, *Ok guys, the reason you haven't caught anything is because you aren't supposed to be fishermen anymore. You're now working for me, so it's time to get rid of your nets.* Instead, he chooses to bless a hard night's work.

If Jesus is interested in a night of fishing, he's likewise interested in a hard day at the office. Whatever our daily work, he values our work enough to act as our personal consultant.

> The truth is that Jesus knows much, much more about your little situation than you give him credit for.
>
> We should not hesitate for one second to ask Jesus to help us with our jobs, because he obviously wants to be involved. Sometimes he may even surprise us with a big catch, followed by a lovely brunch to celebrate.[5]

Women especially need to hear that God values our work. We talk about the qualities of a godly woman in Christian circles, but rarely do we discuss these qualities in the context of work. The result? Modern working women often divorce their spiritual lives from their work. If you haven't noticed, young professional women aren't exactly flooding our churches. In fact, many of them are staying away from church because they think Christians are out of touch with their lives.

Single professional women I meet sometimes feel like second-class citizens in the church. We exalt motherhood and homemaking but often forget that a new generation of women needs a dialogue that values their faith and their work—a dialogue that speaks into their culture. They look around for mentors and support networks and often find such resources outside the church.[6]

Many of the mature career women in my circles don't have time for church. Plus, they don't want to feel judged—especially if they don't fit the mold of a traditional, "religous" woman. Some of them downplay their success in business in order to "fit in" to Christian circles. They too are thirsting for a different dialogue and mentors who value their work.

Jesus is the only mentor I know who bridges these gaps. He isn't about roles or tradition. Regardless of age and stage, he can relate. He doesn't have one plan for twenty-somethings and a different plan for empty nesters. He doesn't even have a different plan for men and women. He works beyond culture, gender, and socioeconomic status.

We see how Jesus values Mary and Martha—they are hardly a traditional, functional family. Mary has a sinful past, and Martha overcompensates as the workaholic and head of household. There is no apparent male leadership in this home. Yet these women are drawn to Jesus, and he is drawn to them. He values them for who they are—not for what they can do for him. He doesn't tell Martha to stop working and settle down with a respectable man. Instead, he meets her right where she is. He speaks to her boldly and calls her to action, and he values her work in the process.

Similarly, the New Testament church empowers women like Lydia and Priscilla. One is single; the other is married. One is geographically planted; the other is constantly relocating. Both are leaders in the church. Neither fits a mold or follows a formula. Both are valued for their work.

What would happen if women today could see just how much Jesus values our work?

JESUS THE SAVIOR: TRANSFORMING WORK

Jesus doesn't just model and value work, he transforms work. This truly sets him apart and makes the gospel message "good news." Jesus knows that we don't just need a change—we need a transformation in our work.

Yet Jesus doesn't expect us to be spiritual orphans. We have a host of mentors—working women of the Bible who have gone before us and give us hope and strength. And we have something better than a job coach. Jesus gives us himself.

Jesus is the classic mentor. He doesn't get stuck in his job as a carpenter, and he isn't afraid to change careers. His time has come. It is time to move on. Mary nudges him, and in his first public miracle he turns the water into wine. There is no turning back. His hardest and most important work is in front of him. It will cost him everything. He leaves his comfortable, stable work as a carpenter and sets out to redeem the world. In doing so, he doesn't just redeem our sin, he redeems our work!

This is where the rubber hits the road. Where Jesus offers something different. He doesn't just tell us to try harder and harder until we get it right. In fact he tells us it's okay to let go.

Stop trying.

Start trusting.

On first blush, this seems all wrong. It cuts against our American work ethic and individual determination. Is Jesus anti-work? Is he telling us to be lazy?

Just the opposite. The gospel message is a message of work. It isn't a license to screw up or get it wrong. It's an invitation to get it right every time. No strings attached. Jesus has already completed the most important work of all, and he allows us to join him, without putting our necks on the line. He has a plan to redeem our work, and he starts by redeeming us first.

> For God so loved the world that he gave his one
> and only Son, that whoever believes in him shall
> not perish but have eternal life.[7]

It's good news. It even sounds too good to be true. God gives us Jesus and provides a way for eternal life. But too often we stop here and see Jesus' work on the cross only as a provision for the next life. Yet in dealing with our sin—the broken part of our work—the gospel squarely deals with us *and our work* in this life. Work doesn't have to be a four-letter word. Our work can be redeemed. Right here. Right now.

※ ※ ※

As we reflect on the working women of the Bible, we notice a common thread. God repeatedly offers a new beginning in their work. Starting with Eve, God delights in giving women a second chance to make things right. To be transformed. To put away the old and make something new. To redeem and even transform work. God keeps his promise to Eve.

Which means God likewise keeps his promise to us.